"In this volume, Catherine Vincie invites the reader to theologically delve deeper as she promotes the church's position on the relationship between science and religion, which is one of harmony. She encourages all to encounter the Holy as she names the right relationship of the human with God and all of creation while offering antidotes to challenge hubris' narrow views on the subject."

Very Rev. David G. Caron, OP
Aquinas Institute of Theology

"Postmodern consciousness locates our Christian community on a small planet earth within a vast expanding universe. Postmodern Christian theology invites us to recognize the post-resurrection cosmic Christ at the heart of this universe. Unfortunately, the church's sacramental and liturgical life-world is not yet attuned to this contemporary thought-world, and Vincie dares to name and explore this challenge to the praying church. What she offers her readers is not a clear resolution of a self-evident problem but rather the gift of a serious question for a renewing Christian liturgy."

Mary Collins, OSB
Mount St. Scholastica, Atchison, Kansas
Professor Emerita, The Catholic University of America

Worship and the New Cosmology

Liturgical and Theological Challenges

Catherine Vincie, RSHM

A Michael Glazier Book

LITURGICAL PRESS
Collegeville, Minnesota

www.litpress.org

A Michael Glazier Book published by Liturgical Press

Cover design by Stefan Killen Design. Cover photo © Thinkstock.

1	2	3	4	5	6	7	8	9

Library of Congress Cataloging-in-Publication Data

Vincie, Catherine, 1951–
   Worship and the new cosmology : liturgical and theological challenges / Catherine Vincie, RSHM.
      pages   cm
   "A Michael Glazier book."
   Includes index.
   ISBN 978-0-8146-8272-2 — ISBN 978-0-8146-8297-5 (ebook)
      1. Religion and science.   2. Worship.   I. Title.

BL240.3.V56   2014
261.5'5—dc23

2014010616

Contents

Preface

Every generation has its challenges in life and in faith. If anything can characterize the emerging spirituality of our day, it is the desire for wholeness—taking every aspect of human life seriously as a revelation of God to us and as a means for us to respond to the living God. No longer are we content to speak of our "spiritual" lives as if our spirit were separate from our bodies, our emotions, and our intellect. Not all of us succeed in such efforts of integration, but we are convinced as never before that a holistic approach to our faith life is required. If we are becoming more aware of our bodies and emotions, we are likewise becoming more aware of the need to reduce the intellectual dissonance between our daily lives and our lives of faith. In our day, the advances in the hard sciences are providing the most challenging area of development for us to integrate into our faith life.

This book is a beginning effort to look at the growing conversation between theologians and scientists, and to apply it to our liturgical life. Systematic theologians of the last twenty years have entered this dialogue with promising results. Theologies of creation, God, Christology, and Pneumatology are all receiving attention as we struggle to integrate the New Science of cosmology and quantum physics with our belief system. At the same time, small faith communities have been taking the New Universe Story into account as they gather for prayer in retreats and workshops. At the moment, very few of these developments have found their way into the official worship of the Christian churches. As a liturgical scholar of the Roman Catholic community, I feel an obligation to bring into dialogue the work of systematic theologians, the worship of these small faith communities, and the official worship of my community. I see this as important because not bringing the New Cosmology into our official worship runs a twofold risk: it risks alienating further those who are already on the fringes of the church, and it risks increasing intellectual dissonance for those living in a scientifically informed world and worshiping with a liturgical tradition that is increasingly out of touch with the development of contemporary science.

Accordingly, in chapter 1, I explore the challenge of the New Cosmology and possible approaches to the science/religion dialogue. In chapter 2, I briefly set out the New Universe Story at the macro and micro levels so as to give a hint of the new developments. Chapters 3, 4, and 5 are a more fulsome exposition of the work of some major theologians who are addressing this issue. Chapters 6 and 7 explore the liturgical implications of this work in terms of sacramental theology and specific worship experiences. I review some liturgical work that has already been done, and present some of my own beginning efforts to create new prayers and new patterns of worship.

Adapting our current liturgical books to integrate the New Science will take many years and will require the work of many scholars and many faith communities who are already experimenting with new prayer forms. I invite your consideration on these issues, and look forward to the dialogue required to bring this integration into reality.

Acknowledgments

"God, Who Stretched the Spangled Heavens." Words: Catherine Cameron. © 1967 Hope Publishing Company, Carol Stream, IL 60188. All rights reserved. Used by permission.

"Spirit Blowing through Creation" by Marty Haugen. Copyright © 1987 by GIA Publications, Inc. 7404 S. Mason Ave., Chicago, IL 60638. www.giamusic.com. 800.442.1358. All rights reserved. Used by permission.

"Mother Earth, Our Birthing Mother" by Norman Habel in *Habel Hymns 1: Songs for Celebrating with Creation*. Copyright © 2004 by Norman C. Habel. All rights reserved. Used by permission of Willow Publishing.

Excerpt from Arthur Peacocke, *Paths from Science towards God: The End of All Our Exploring* (Oxford, UK: Oneworld, 2011), 1–2. All rights reserved. Used by permission.

Excerpts from © Nan C. Merrill, 2008, *Psalms for Praying: An Invitation to Wholeness*, Continuum US, by permission of Bloomsbury Publishing Inc.

Part I

Science and Religion in Dialogue

In the twenty-first century, we live in a world that has contesting truth claims about reality. Science and religion, for example, seem to have opposing ways of relating to reality that appear to cancel one another out. Some scientists would insist that one must leave one's religious faith "at the door" of the laboratory. It is not unusual to hear that one cannot be a scientist and a believer at the same time. Science can verify its truth claims, they would say, while religion cannot. Therefore if one were to put science up against religion on a given issue, the scientific answer inevitably wins. On the other hand, some religionists would say that science itself can fall into a kind of faith (scientism), that is, the belief that science is the only approach to truth that holds any legitimacy—an idea they must reject. It is a question, then, of competing truth or faith claims. Still other religionists (biblical literalists, for example) would say that both science and religion are after the same quest for truth, but in that contest between science and faith, faith wins and the scientific answers must be rejected. If one wants to worship, one must leave the insights of the scientific community "at the door" of the church.

But what happens in the church communities that are unwilling to accept the absolute contrast or contradiction between their faith and science? What if science and religion have something legitimate to offer one another? What do mainline Christian churches do with the insights of a scientific community that has brought tremendously new and exciting insights into the universe at the micro or macro levels? Must we live schizophrenic lives, believing and worshiping with one cosmology expressed in doctrines, prayers, or hymns while standing in amazement and appreciation at the pictures from the Hubble Space Telescope that indicate that in the known universe there are over 200 billion galaxies? Will the two worlds ever meet?

Chapter 1

The Challenge of the New Cosmology

Periodically, key new insights into the workings of the world reach a tipping point and cause a radical shift in cultural sensibilities. Even if the changes occur in one field of human endeavor, certain developments are of such consequence that their effects ripple out across the whole social spectrum. When this happens, the natural and social sciences, philosophy, theology, and the arts share the burden of adapting to the new insights and reconfiguring the human imagination in light of them.[1]

We are, I will argue, at one of these historic moments, when, ready or not, we are challenged to integrate a new cosmology and an ecological consciousness into our thought, our lives, our work. This new cosmology has implications for our understanding of God, the universe, and humanity's place in it. It involves not only how we live but how we will pray as individuals and as communities. How are we to understand the magnitude of such a change in consciousness, and what are the implications for Christian theology and liturgy?

Shifts in consciousness do not happen in a day, nor is one person singlehandedly responsible for the insights that foster the emergence of such a shift. However, there are key figures and formative centuries

[1] Parts of this chapter are taken from my vice-presidential address to the North American Academy of Liturgy in 2011. It is published as "Praying with the New Cosmology," *Proceedings of the North American Academy of Liturgy Annual Meeting*, San Francisco, CA, January 6–9, 2011, 3–16.

that usher in a new vision of reality. Writing in 1992, Ewert Cousins proposed that we are at a major new epic in human consciousness.[2] He expressed it in Karl Jaspers's term of being at a second Axial Period in human history. By that he meant that we can understand human consciousness as generally divided into three major periods: a pre-Axial Period, the first Axial Period, and the second Axial Period. The pre-Axial Period, dating from the rise of hominids to roughly 800 BCE, was characterized as a world inhabited by tribal peoples who lived in harmony with nature, had a collective consciousness, and expressed themselves in mythic language and ritual.

The first Axial Period was from 800 to 200 BCE, peaking in 500 BCE when, Cousins argues, there was "a striking transformation of consciousness [that] occurred around the world in three geographic regions, apparently without the influence of one on the other."[3] In China two great teachers emerged, Lao-tze and Confucius; in India the Vedas were superseded by the Upanishads; Buddha and Mahavira were instrumental in forming two new religious traditions; Zoroaster emerged in Persia, while in Israel the major prophets exercised significant influence. Finally in Greece, what we know as Greek philosophy developed under the leadership of Socrates, Plato, and Aristotle, among many others. This first Axial Period was a transition from tribal to individual consciousness that was self-reflective, analytic of natural and social phenomena, and addressed the individual spiritual journey into the divine. As with all periods of transition, something was lost as well as gained in this period. The negative side of the shift in consciousness was a loss in the organic relationship with nature and a weakening of tribal connections. It tended toward an alienation from our earthly roots with a propensity to look toward heaven and to reject matter in favor of spirit. On the positive side, Cousins suggested that this first Axial Period released an enormous amount of spiritual energy that was best expressed in monasticism, that is, in individuals who could set themselves on the margins of society and take a radical stand vis-à-vis the culture as they progressed on their individual spiritual journeys.[4]

---

[2] Ewert H. Cousins, *Christ of the 21st Century* (Rockport, MA: Element, 1992).
[3] Ibid., 4.
[4] Ibid., 7.

We are, Cousins argues, on the verge of the emergence of a second Axial Period, which began with the Copernican revolution; the transformation of consciousness of our age is that from individual to global consciousness. This global sense leads to a new awareness of unity but without a loss of distinction (in other words, a sense of unity beyond tribal ties that takes the individual into account), and a regrounding in matter and in the earth (in other words, a new appreciation of the material with the addition of cosmic consciousness with its ethical implications). "This new global consciousness," Cousins says, "must be organized ecologically, supported by structures that will ensure justice and peace."[5] Communities in the second Axial Period must also reappropriate the strengths of the pre-Axial Period with those of the first Axial Period and turn these resources to the contemporary problems of our age.

Clearly the world community currently consists of people living with the values of the pre-Axial, first Axial, and second Axial Period all at the same time, but this does not diminish the significance of a movement to a new consciousness that starts small but grows to a critical mass that is perceptible at a global level. In terms of history, if we count Nicolas Copernicus as the instigator of a new view of the universe (1543), we are only in the first five centuries of such an epochal change. How long it will take for this epochal change to reach a global level is uncertain, but the cooperation of peoples from all three periods in the interest of ecological reform suggests that we are well on our way.[6]

I am in agreement with Cousins in his analysis of the transition to different Axial periods, but I think that he did not go far enough in exploring the impact of the New Sciences at the micro and macro levels and the impact of a new cosmic consciousness or a new cosmology on our generation. He does suggest that with the New Cosmology and our experience of space, we are "for the first time . . . actually experiencing the Copernican universe and not merely understanding

---

[5] Ibid., 10.

[6] It is estimated that there are over 20,000 individual groups worldwide engaged in ecological reform. A particularly striking example is the Pachamama Alliance based in Ecuador where indigenous peoples work with those of the developed world on ecological renewal. See http://www.pachamama.org.

it intellectually with the aid of an abstract model of the solar system."[7] This is a significant moment which has vast implications for religious experience, theology, and worship. Because of the close ties between cosmic and religious models, Cousins claims "this new experience of space will open new varieties of religious experience and give new meaning to cosmological symbols."[8] This is an extremely provocative statement which begs further exploration. Cousins does not explore this line of reasoning, but it is one that I hope to pursue throughout this book.

Thus far we have used the words cosmic and cosmology without defining them and it is time to do so now. What is a cosmology? In short, a cosmology is how human persons experience themselves in relation to the cosmos. It is the lens through which reality is viewed and interpreted. A cosmology tells you how things are in reality, what really matters, and provides the foundation for core values, belief systems, and moral norms. A cosmology gives a community meaning and purpose.

What characterized the cosmology of the first Axial Period was the fact that the human story was treated in an isolated manner and located in a static world. The creation stories that came out of the Axial world, of which the biblical account is one, posited the creation of humanity in a finished cosmos that was between four and five thousand years old. This was all to change in the post-Copernican, Modern Period.

The Modern Age (roughly from 1600 CE to the mid-1900s) saw a vast change in the cosmology of the Western world and, as Brian Swimme and Thomas Berry have noted, it needed to displace a long list of assumptions:

> that the celestial bodies were made of material different from the matter of the Earth and follow different physical laws in their movement;
>
> that celestial movements must be circular;
>
> that Earth was only some five thousand years old;

---

[7] Cousins, *Christ*, 50.
[8] Ibid.

that the various species of plants and animals were fixed in the beginning;

that the universe was best understood as a great chain of being in hierarchical arrangements;

that humans were placed on the Earth as a temporary setting for their spiritual development;

that the most reliable source of understanding was to follow the teachings of the ancients rather than the observable evidence of the present.[9]

Because of the work of Copernicus and Galileo, the earth lost its centrality as the sun took over that position in our solar system. The relationship between humankind and nature also changed in the Modern Period. The world became understood as a vast machine over which humanity ruled. Humanity lived not with other subjects, but in a universe of objects over which we assumed more and more power and with which we had less and less a relationship. The Enlightenment brought about an understanding of the human as one who has critical reason, able through empirical observation to come to scientific knowledge. Isaac Newton's discoveries led to an explosion of technology in the Industrial Revolution, which freed Western culture from many of the burdens of human life but at a significant cost. Exploitation of the environment was the price paid for vast economic growth.

Granting the significant developments of the sixteenth century, we can speak about the New Cosmology as that which emerged in the mid-1800s and continues into the present. We cannot underestimate the impact of Charles Darwin and colleagues in their insight into the evolutionary nature of Earth and its inhabitants. Rather than a fixed notion of reality, their work suggested that we and all creatures of Earth developed gradually in an irreversible movement from simplicity to greater and greater complexity. We humans, they tell us, are related to all that came before and truly are Earth come to consciousness. What we will become is, as yet, unknown.

---

[9] Brian Swimme and Thomas Berry, *The Universe Story* (San Francisco: Harper, 1992), 228.

In the twentieth century, through the work of scientists like Albert Einstein and Edwin Hubble, our perception of the world enlarged beyond the earth and our solar system to a much greater appreciation of the size and complexity of the universe. Hubble discovered there were other galaxies besides our own Milky Way; that was only the beginning of a vast series of discoveries at the macro and micro levels. Through the new sciences of astronomy and astrophysics, we are able to ask questions not just about the age and development of humanity or even of Earth, but the age and development of the known universe. We learned that time does not begin with the age of Earth, but with the first flaring forth in minute fractions of a second after there was nothing in what has become known as the "Big Bang." Space is not limited to what we can see with the human eye, but what our most developed observatories can learn about nebulas, stars, and galaxies from the electromagnetic echo they leave behind. Since Einstein and his theory of general relativity, we have come to realize that space, time, and mass are related and that the universe is expanding.

This knowledge has great implications for our self-understanding and our understanding of the world and our place within it. Rather than being a completed and static universe, the New Cosmology suggests that the universe is expanding in a sequence of irreversible evolutionary events of which humanity is a part. The human story cannot be told any longer within Earth's story; the human story is only comprehensible in the story of an expanding and evolutionary universe. The universe story is our story. As Swimme and Berry tell us, "we live not so much in a cosmos as in a cosmogenesis, a cosmogenesis best presented in narrative; scientific in its data, mythic in its form."[10]

In 1962 the historian of science Thomas Kuhn published a work that would prove to have significant value both to the scientific community and to many other fields as well. It was titled *The Structure of Scientific Revolutions*, and presented a way of understanding the development of modern science. In it, Kuhn introduced the term "paradigm shift" to speak of the revolutionary change that, in his analysis, marked contemporary science. For Kuhn, a paradigm was

[10] Ibid., 229.

"the entire constellation of beliefs, values, techniques, and so on shared by the members of a given community."[11] This constellation (of beliefs, etc.) is so taken for granted by the practitioners that it is seen as the only legitimate way of conceiving the world. With time, however, anomalies develop in the use of the paradigm that beg for alternative strategies. For Kuhn, this creates a crisis in the community that steadily grows until practitioners lose faith in the existing paradigm and seek a new one that more adequately addresses the anomalies in the system. Kuhn suggests using the term "paradigm shift" to describe that movement from one set of theoretical rules and methods that no longer answer all the problems of normal science to a new set of rules and methods that are simply more successful than their competitors. Kuhn's contribution has been to give us language to speak of broad-based change in methodology and content of many fields, and I would like to apply it here for my purposes.

While it is possible to speak of the theory of paradigm shifts with equanimity, it is quite another thing to be involved in the actual crisis that precipitates a paradigm shift itself. Faith in the new model does not come quickly or easily. Nicolas Copernicus threatened to turn his culture on its head with his heliocentric cosmology that decentered the earth as the hub of the universe. However, at the time of its publication in 1543 and until 1700, his theory was rejected by most scientists on physical as well as theological grounds. Regarding the latter, it appeared that his heliocentric universe contradicted scripture.

In hindsight such criticism can be seen as ludicrous, but at the moment of new discoveries, the science in question is neither obviously correct nor constructive. To the contrary, it seems to subvert what is taken for granted as the way things really are. Major paradigm shifts cause seismic trembling in the whole cultural world of a society. Identity comes under assault. One's stability is upset; one's sense of balance is jarred; one is thrust into a period of uncertainty because the implications of the new paradigm are not at all clear. In fact, the full implications may take tens or even hundreds of years to work completely through the social system. Social disorientation may occur;

---

[11] Thomas Kuhn, *The Structure of Scientific Revolutions* (Chicago: The University of Chicago Press, 1996), 175.

rebellion at the changes can be a result. The seventeenth-century poet John Donne wrote eloquently of the disorientation he experienced as a result of the work of Copernicus and Galileo.

> And new Philosophy calls all in doubt,
> The Element of fire is quite put out;
> The sun is lost, and th' earth, and no man's wit
> Can well direct him, where to looke for it. . . .
> 'Tis all in pieces, all coherence gone;
> All just supply, and all Relation. . . .
> For the world's beauty is decayed, or gone,
> Beauty, that's color, and proportion.[12]

Not all feel as negatively about paradigm shifts as Donne, of course. A degree of excitement may develop as the culture sets aside the limits of older frameworks and reshapes more adequate new ones. In reality, uncertainty, instability, disorientation, excitement, and confidence might all be experienced at the same time within any single culture.

I am suggesting that we, as a culture, are facing in this second Axial Period perhaps the most challenging paradigm shift to date due to the developments in the new sciences, especially those of the last 150 years. Advances in genetics, paleontology, cosmology, astrophysics, quantum mechanics, evolutionary biology, and particle physics have all contributed to a radically new way of seeing the world and our place within it. The result is a New Cosmology. The current ecological crisis is one aspect that is addressed by the New Cosmology—the climate change debate exemplifies the struggle over a new paradigm. Our religious traditions have yet or are just beginning to take cognizance of these new studies, and as Cousins remarks, "religion cannot merely draw from their resources as they exist in the first Axial Period, but must transform them in light of the second Axial Period."[13] That is the seemingly overwhelming agenda that we are facing at the moment. At the level of faith, belief, religious experience, ritual expression, and theological reflection, we are called to save what is the best

---

[12] *The Complete Poetry of John Donne*, ed. J. T. Shawcross, The Anchor-Seventeenth Century Series (New York: Doubleday Anchor, 1967), 271–86; esp. 277–78. As quoted in Zachary Hayes, *A Window to the Divine* (Quincy, IL: Franciscan Press, 1997), 3.

[13] Cousins, *Christ*, 11.

of our tradition while revising and expanding our horizons in light of the epochal change of the second Axial Period.

This is the challenge of the New Science and the New Cosmology at this time. It is important to note that this new story does not of itself supplant other stories that have guided humanity over the millennia. "It is rather a case of providing a more comprehensive context in which all these earlier stories discover in themselves a new validity and a more expansive role."[14] It is our generation of believers who must integrate this new paradigm shift of the second Axial Period into the way we see the world, our place in it, and our religious traditions. While the Genesis creation myth was an expressive model in which persons showed forth their religious experience, it is we who must either retrieve or create new expressive models for our religious experience and consequently rethink questions of the Triune God, creation, salvation, and redemption. Where will we find these models, or must they be created anew? Cousins suggests that we need especially to retrieve and reappropriate the symbolic thinking of the people of the pre-Axial Period and, in particular, their relationship and rootedness in the earth. We in the second Axial Period must plunge ourselves back into matter and rediscover its spiritual significance. "It is," he suggests, "precisely in symbols and in the exercise of our symbolic imagination that this significance is manifest."[15] I would suggest, in addition, that it is in the images from space, in particular from the Hubble Telescope, that we are finding new images that are engendering new religious experiences. On the other hand, new religious experiences are finding expression in the images of the New Cosmology.

Liturgical scholars and theologians must explore the prayer of our communities to see how we might worship the living God in light of this newly articulated Cosmogenesis and the religious experience it engenders, even while our systematic theologians are rethinking our whole belief system. Liturgical scholars are not only scholars of what our religious traditions have done in the past and present. Some of us are responsible for the formation and modifications of denominational prayer books and ritual materials that will shape our traditions for years to come. What difference do the New Cosmology and the

---

[14] Swimme and Berry, *The Universe Story*, 238.
[15] Cousins, *Christ*, 32.

ecological crisis make to us as we shape new prayers and symbols for the Christian community? To suggest that the culture is experiencing a major paradigm shift in this second Axial Period and that we would remain untouched by it seems naïve, even irresponsible. This book is a tentative step in exploring the ramifications of this paradigm shift for liturgy.

Questions of Method

Science and Religion

As we begin our discussion of the relationship between science and theology, it is important to address how theology is to relate to ever new scientific discoveries. It is clear that theology cannot simply affirm each new scientific discovery or theory as they unfold—these are subject to change as new data and new technologies emerge. It is also true that in a tradition such as Roman Catholicism—one that has always affirmed the place of understanding and intelligibility in our faith—the quest for truth by all fields of endeavor should have a place at the table of theological discourse. We cannot simply go forward blithely oblivious to the evolving insights of our scientific community. It is thus appropriate at this time to address the various ways in which religion and science have been or could be related.

Theologian of science and religion John Haught has clarified the situation by proposing four possible ways of relating the two fields. The summary which follows is based on his text *Science and Religion: From Conflict to Conversation*.[16] He suggests that in recent history (the last five hundred years) there indeed has been a stormy relationship between the two (e.g., the controversy between Copernicus, Galileo, and the church, and the more recent religious protests against evolutionary theory), but that the relationship between the two fields is more complex than one of mere opposition. In fact, there is a range of possibilities for how science and religion interact. It will be helpful to spell out in some detail each of these possibilities.

---

[16] John Haught, *Science and Religion: From Conflict to Conversation* (Mahwah, NJ: Paulist Press, 1995), especially chapter 1. For a slightly different interpretation see Ian Barbour, *Religion in an Age of Science* (San Francisco: Harper & Row, 1990).

Conflict

In light of the scientific revolution of Copernicus and Galileo, many people, scientists and religionists alike, would suggest that the two are in irreconcilable *conflict* with one another. Part of this conflict lies in the ability of science to demonstrate the truth of its ideas while religion cannot. Science can test to see if its theories are in fact "falsifiable," but religious positions are "untestable." For some scientists this means that religion is in conflict with science and that one cannot be both a scientist and a person of faith. From another perspective, biblical literalists (those who take the Bible as being literally true) also see conflict between the two fields and argue that the Bible is right while scientifically developed theories such as evolution are wrong. Still others would argue that science is the enemy of religion, that "it was the coming of science that caused most of the emptiness and meaninglessness in modern life and culture."[17] Since one of the main functions of religion is to provide meaning in life, the scientific argument for life's meaninglessness puts science and religion in irreconcilable conflict.

Contrast

Not all believers or scientists are so adamantly convinced that there exists a hopelessly conflictual relationship between science and religion. Some argue that *contrast* can and ought to characterize the relationship. In the contrast argument, science and religion are understood to operate in different arenas. Each has a distinct content and task, and it would not make any sense to compare the two. Followers of this position are content to allow each to maintain its own silo existence and in so doing, all will be well. It is an understandable effort to avoid conflict, but Haught argues that there are several problems with the contrast position.

First, there is a danger of *conflation* in this approach into which both scientists and religionists can fall. The danger is that the distinctions between the two fields are lost—science and religion are conflated into one another in such a way that their differences are not honored.

---

[17] Haught, *Science and Religion*, 11–12.

The different content, agendas, and methods of the two fields are not taken into account. Conflation is as much in evidence today as in the time of Galileo, when the church argued that a heliocentric universe contradicted Scripture. The church failed to recognize that the Bible was not a scientific book, and that science had the right to propose a different cosmology without threatening the unique insights of biblical religion. Contemporary believers who conflate science and religious belief on the question of creation call such fusion "creation science." Such persons in the United States have fought to introduce a biblical literalist interpretation of the creation of the world into school curriculums to counter the scientific findings of evolution that are being taught.

A second danger in the contrast position is that it does not take sufficiently into account the presuppositions of science (its "faith," if you will). This is also a problem of conflation, in that now scientists conflate their findings with their "faith" that science is the only method for learning about the universe or seeking truth. Rather than describing this as pure science, Haught argues that this is a philosophical view that he calls "scientism."[18]

A third danger within the contrast position is the effort at *concordism*. This is the attempt to "force[s] the biblical text to correspond, at least in a loose way, with the contours of modern cosmology."[19] For example, some religious scientists try to relate the six biblical days of creation with six epochs of world history.[20] It is an attempt to make the Bible look scientifically respectable as well as to avoid conflict, but what appears to be at least superficial agreement begins to unravel as new scientific theories develop.

Haught suggests that while the approach of contrast is in many ways attractive, it fails on two accounts. First, it does not keep the two fields distinct so that genuine conversation that respects the differences between the two fields may be had. Consequently, it does not take into account the possibilities of science and religion actually cooperating with one another.

---

[18] Ibid., 16.

[19] Ibid., 13.

[20] Ibid., 14. Haught argues that physicist Gerald Schroeder does this in his book *Genesis and the Big Bang*.

Contact and Conversation

If conflict and contrast are problematic paths of relating science and religion, it would seem that *contact* would be an attractive alternative. This position does not allow the two fields to simply coexist in isolated parallel columns, but seeks to relate one to the other. An important part of this approach suggests that religion and theology cannot remain oblivious to what is happening in science, but "must seek to express its ideas in terms that take the best of science into account lest it become intellectually irrelevant."[21] Perhaps the best way to understand the dynamic here is *conversation*. Each field preserves its identity, but the practitioners seek to remain in contact or relationship with each other. This approach proposes that scientific discoveries can be helpful in opening up new vistas for faith in ways that were not possible before. We might also say that science can help religious faith to flourish in new ways, even as religion can help science not to exceed its boundaries in truth seeking.

Confirmation

Haught suggests that it is tempting to remain at the level of contact, but that this does not go far enough. He posits that "religion is in a very deep way supportive of the entire scientific enterprise."[22] By this he means that the presupposition of religion that the universe is intelligible is the very foundation of science's approach to understanding reality. Thus religion would support or *confirm* science in its quest for truth or unifying knowledge. Religion would not unequivocally affirm or deny any particular scientific explanation of reality since these are constantly being modified and expanded, but it would support science's effort to seek reality's overall rationality. Religion, however, makes its own contribution to the search for truth. Religious myths, stories, and symbols point to an intelligibility that exceeds even our best efforts at scientific understanding, thus holding out an infinite horizon to the finite efforts of our scientific explorations.

[21] Ibid., 18.
[22] Ibid., 21.

Throughout this text I will be using Haught's taxonomy in that I will be speaking of how contemporary theologians are using the New Science and the New Cosmology to recast the expressions of faith that are ours. I am suggesting that contact and confirmation are the only reasonable ways consistent with Catholic epistemology to explore the relationship of science and religion. In addition to the relationship between science and religion, we also must address the relationship between theology and liturgy. It is to that topic that we now turn.

Lex Orandi, Lex Credendi

Anyone who has read in the field of liturgical theology during the past fifty years knows that the Latin tag *lex orandi, lex credendi* (law of prayer, law of belief) has been at the heart of the debate on liturgical methodology.[23] Authors, such as Alexander Schmemann, Aidan Kavanagh, Geoffery Wainwright, Edward Kilmartin, Mary Collins, among many others, have debated the merits and implications of putting the accent on prayer or on belief, on whether prayer *founds* belief or the other way around, on whether there is a difference between *founding* and *influencing*. Some have placed almost an exclusive emphasis on prayer founding belief (such as Odo Casel and Aidan Kavanagh). Others have argued that the lack of verb in this phrase allows one to easily invert the phrase "prayer establishes belief" to "belief establishes prayer." In fact, Pope Pius XII used the latter in his encyclical *Mediator Dei* to counter what he felt was an excessive emphasis on prayer without enough attention to doctrine

---

[23] Alexander Schmemann, *Introduction to Liturgical Theology*, 2nd ed. (New York: St Vladimir's Seminary Press, 1975); Aidan Kavanagh, *On Liturgical Theology* (New York: Pueblo, 1984); Edward Foley, Kathleen Hughes, Gilbert Ostdiek, "The Preparatory Rites: A Case Study in Liturgical Ecology," in *The Ecological Challenge: Ethical, Liturgical, and Spiritual Responses*, ed. Richard N. Fragomeni and John T. Pawlikowski (Collegeville, MN: Michael Glazier/Liturgical Press, 1994), 84. See also Edward Kilmartin, "Theology as Theology of the Liturgy," chap. 6, *Christian Liturgy: Theology and Practice*, vol. 1 (Kansas City: Sheed & Ward, 1988); Geoffrey Wainwright, *Doxology: The Praise of God in Worship, Doctrine and Life; A Systematic Theology* (New York: Oxford University Press, 1980); Mary Collins, "Critical Questions for Liturgical Theology," *Worship* 53, no. 4 (July 1979): 302–17.

and scripture as sources for Christian life.[24] The original statement of the fifth-century author Prosper of Aquitaine is technically "*ut legem credenda lex statuat supplicandi.*" It means explicitly "let the law of praying establish the law of believing," but not all liturgical theologians understand this phrase in the precise and limited way that Prosper originally intended it.[25]

In most recent references to the Latin phrase, what is meant is that the law of prayer is the *foundation* for the law of belief. Consciousness of this relationship has led contemporary scholars to a whole new appreciation of the liturgical life of the church as expressive of the community's encounter with the living God (and thus *theologia prima*) and as a locus for theological reflection (*theologia secunda*).[26] If you want to know the faith of a given ecclesial community, observe and study the principal liturgies of the church year, letting the liturgies be your point of departure for theological reflection. While these discussions have been a way to treat what constitutes authentic liturgical theology as a methodological question, I would like to take a step back from that debate, and reflect upon the dynamic between the development of the liturgy and the development of doctrine/theology. After two thousand years of Christian living, liturgy, and theological reflection, I do not believe that we are in the position of saying that the community's prayer always is the root of its theological reflection as some scholars would have us believe. The simultaneity of religious experience and its celebration in expressive prayer forms (liturgy) and reflection on that liturgical experience in light of tradition (theology) suggests that we need to reconsider the relationship between the law of prayer and the law of belief once again. I do not want to settle the debate on which *founds* which. I would rather explore the *influence* of doctrine and secondary theology on the liturgy.

[24] *AAS* 39 (1947): 540: "Lex credenda legem statuit supplicandi."

[25] Although the phrase is stated in different ways by different authors, this is its formulation in Migne, *Patrologia Latina* vol. 50: col. 555. See P. De Clerk, " 'Lex orandi-Lex credendi': The Original Sense and Historical Avatars of an Equivocal Adage," *Studia Liturgica* 24 (1994): 178–200, for an analysis on the original meaning of this adage.

[26] See especially the work of Aidan Kavanagh, *On Liturgical Theology*.

Historically it can be shown that doctrine has shaped the church's worship practice.[27] Geoffrey Wainwright claims that while Protestant-ism exhibits the clearest example of doctrine controlling worship, Roman Catholicism has also engaged in a reciprocal shaping of worship and doctrine.[28] Think, for example, of how the struggles with Arianism influenced liturgical prayer; the doxology "Glory be to the Father *through* the Son and *in* the Holy Spirit" was rewritten as "Glory be to the Father *with* (*meta*) the Son, together *with* (*sūn*) the Holy Spirit" to erase any suggestion of subordinationism. At other times the magisterium has acted to modify worship such as inserting the Nicene-Constantinopolitan creed into the eucharistic liturgy. At still other points, the church reshaped its liturgy to take into account changes in Marian doctrine (which itself flowed from the commu-nity's religious experience and piety). Here doctrine clearly had a hand in keeping the church's prayer orthodox as doctrine developed.

But there are other instances when theological reflection that is not at the level of official doctrine has also left its mark on the church's liturgy. Creative members of the church community brought their talents to bear in bringing new theological developments and new expressions of Christian piety into the liturgy. Consider, for example, the thousands of sequences that were added to the eucharist in the medieval church. These poetic texts were not in the form of what we would call "second theology." They were expressive forms of piety and belief that were influenced by "second theology," among other things. Through these sequences, not only doctrine but systematic theology and piety had an influence on Christian liturgy.[29] From another point of view, while we can acknowledge Kavanagh's con-cern that liturgy is the primary place of the church's encountering God and doing its corporate business in light of God's offer of rela-

---

[27] See Geoffrey Wainwright, *Doxology*. For a consideration of Wainwright's work, see David W. Fagerberg, *What Is Liturgical Theology? A Study in Methodology* (College-ville, MN: Pueblo/Liturgical Press, 1992), 102–36.

[28] Wainwright, *Doxology*, 263.

[29] Here I want to suggest that Aidan Kavanagh is correct in arguing that prayer *founds* belief. I would also want to expand on his suggestion that doctrine/theology *influences* liturgy—something which he does not pursue but which I intend to. See *On Liturgical Theology*, 92.

tionship, we also need to take into account that the liturgy is not the only place where the community encounters the Holy One; nor is liturgy the only place where reflection on faith happens. My interest is precisely at this point.

I am interested in asking the question of what difference the New Science and the New Cosmology is making or could make to our religious experience and to recent developments in systematic theology. That is a first step; a second step is to ask what difference these theological developments might make to Christian worship. Liturgy has always taken place within the context of a given cosmology; often that cosmology is taken for granted as the only possible way of conceiving the world and finds uncritical inclusion in the whole liturgical act (inclusive of prayers, music, art, architecture, etc.). As we have indicated above, at this second Axial Period we are at a major paradigm shift to a new cosmology, and the question of how the church might be in prayer in light of this paradigm shift needs to be addressed.

Chapter 2

The New Science and the Story of the Cosmos

Before setting out the implications of a contact or confirmation approach between theology and science, it will be helpful to summarize what the New Science of the last 150 years is teaching us about the universe. As we said earlier, a cosmology is a lens through which to view reality; it helps us to understand who we are and how we fit into the universe. As Brian Swimme and Thomas Berry noted, "cosmology aims at articulating the story of the universe so that humans can enter fruitfully into the web of relationships within the Universe."[1]

For as long as humans have existed, they have sought ways to understand the universe and the place of human beings in it, and have found means to express those beliefs. In the pre-Axial Period cosmologies were found in myths and rituals or were expressed in art chiseled or drawn in rock caves or carved on human bodies in a process called scarification. In the first Axial Period, we find in Genesis two cosmological stories (Gen 1:1ff. and Gen 2:4ff.) for the Ancient Israelites that posit a Creator and the birth of creation at a given period of time some four to five thousand years ago. It was a fixed cosmology with the understanding that individual species in-

---

[1] Brian Swimme and Thomas Berry, *The Universe Story* (San Francisco: Harper, 1992), 23.

cluding humankind were created complete at the origin of creation. It is now widely accepted that the Genesis accounts of creation were contextualized within and influenced by other Near Eastern cosmologies such as the Babylonian epic *Enuma Elish* and perhaps other Egyptian accounts of creation as well. The first account from Genesis 1, for example, was written in Babylon to counter the accepted notions of creation current in this area. For Israel, it was the one God who created the world out of chaos for the elect; creation was not the result of the struggle between Marduk and Tiamat of the *Enuma Elish* epic.

As science slowly emerged in Greco-Roman thought, new cosmologies also arose and competed for a place in the culture's imagination. One of the first astronomers to create a numerical system for understanding the universe was Ptolemy, a Greek-speaking Roman citizen who died in Alexandria in 168 CE. His was a static universe that was geocentric and thought to be everlasting. Even while his cosmology was at odds with the Jewish understanding of the role of a Creator and the creation of the world at a certain time, the Ptolemaic universe held sway in the West until the Copernican Revolution in 1543. From our perspective in the twenty-first century, we can call it the "old cosmology." This cosmology was held both by the scientific community and by Christian theologians as the way the world really was, and, together with the biblical cosmology of Genesis, it was integrated in the theological treatises of the time. For the first fifteen centuries, right through the medieval world, theology and cosmology were held as one living whole; there was no separation between the two. Examples can be drawn from Hildegard of Bingen (twelfth century), Bonaventure (thirteenth century), and Thomas Aquinas (thirteenth century).[2] Hildegard wrote in her *summa* of Christian doctrine (*Scivias*) that humans are bound together with the rest of creation. Humans, she said, are "made in a wondrous way with great glory from the dust of the earth, and so intertwined with the strengths of the rest of

---

[2] I am indebted to Elizabeth Johnson for her references to these authors. See her presidential address to the Catholic Theological Society of America, "Turn to the Heavens and the Earth: Retrieval of the Cosmos in Theology," in *Proceedings of the Fifty-First Annual Convention of the CTSA* (June 6–9, 1996), 2–3. See also N. Max Wildiers, *The Theologian and His Universe: Theology and Cosmology from the Middle Ages to the Present*, trans. Paul Dunphy (New York: Seabury Press, 1982), chaps. 1–3; George S. Hendry, *Theology of Nature* (Philadelphia: Westminster Press, 1980), chap. 1.

creation that we can never be separated from them."[3] Bonaventure taught that the universe was a place to see the glory of the Creator. "Whoever is not enlightened by the splendor of created things is blind; whoever is not aroused by the sound of their voice is deaf; whoever does not praise God for all these creatures is mute; whoever after so much evidence does not recognize the First Principle is a fool."[4] Aquinas in his *summa* wrote that "For goodness, which in God is simple and uniform, in creatures is manifold and divided. Thus the whole universe together participates in divine goodness more perfectly, and represents it better, than any single creature whatever."[5] After the Copernican revolution this easy symbiosis between science and religion was lost and *conflict* between the two reigned. It is only in our time that efforts of *contact* and *confirmation* are being felt, even while some of each camp continue to hold that science and religion are irreconcilable.

The New Cosmology

The cosmology of the last 150 years is what we may call mathematical or scientific cosmology. Theories about the birth, evolution, and development of the universe have progressed as new positions by theoretical physicists were put forth and as new scientific instruments for observing the visible universe on the macro and micro levels were developed. Of invaluable importance have been the telescopes we use either on earth or in earth orbit (e.g., the Hubble Space Telescope) that have helped us observe the magnitude of the skies, and the microscopes that have aided our understanding that which is infinitesimally small. The radical discovery that the universe is expanding has changed the questions that science is now seeking to answer. Scientists are focusing on present experience but are also extending their gaze backward in time, outward and inward in space, and deep into the phenomenon of complexity and relationality. They

[3] Hildegard of Bingen, *Scivias*, trans. Mother Columba Hart and Jane Bishop (New York: Paulist, 1980), 94, as quoted in Johnson, "Turn to the Heavens," 2.

[4] Bonaventure, *The Mind's Journey to God*, trans. Lawrence Cunningham (Chicago: Franciscan Herald Press, 1979), as quoted in Johnson, "Turn to the Heavens," 3.

[5] *Summa Theologicae* I, q. 47, a. 1, as quoted in Johnson, "Turn to the Heavens," 3.

are trying to understand what was the origin of the cosmos, such that the seas and mountains on earth exist as they are; why the elemental particles interact as they do, so that the human community can express itself in art forms as diverse as cathedrals, bridges, and opera; how mind has developed from inert matter, so that the human person is both conscious and has self-consciousness. Scientific cosmologists found they have to deal with the extraordinarily old (13.8 billion years); the fantastically large (over 200 billion galaxies with over 100 billion stars in each); and infinitesimally small (matter as small as 10^{-43} microns); and the profoundly complex and interrelated nature of reality. Coming to terms with such a vast enterprise will be demanding in every area of human endeavor, theology included, as science itself invents new language (quarks, neutrinos, dark matter, dark energy) and new mathematical models to comprehend the old, the immense, the small, and the complex. Theologians are at the very beginning of integrating New Science and New Cosmology; our liturgies are farther back still, reflecting the cosmology of the biblical world and of the Ptolemaic cosmos.

The Cosmos as Narrative

As theologian John Haught notes, "One of the most surprising scientific discoveries of the past century and a half is that the universe is an unfolding story. . . . The whole of nature, not just earth and human history, has an essentially narrative character."[6] In other words, we have moved from a static and stable understanding of the cosmos—which served as a backdrop for the unfolding narrative of the Earth and human history with its sorrow, pain and suffering, joy, and promise—to a dynamic and unfolding universe that now frames those same human experiences. As I noted earlier, the New Cosmology suggests that the universe is expanding in a sequence of irreversible evolutionary events of which humanity is a part. The human story cannot be told any longer within Earth's story; the human story is only comprehensible within the story of an expanding and evolutionary universe.

---

[6] John Haught, *Christianity and Science: Toward a Theology of Nature* (Maryknoll, NY: Orbis Books, 2007), xi.

The universe story is our story. If theology is to take science seriously and learn from it for its own purposes, it needs to better appreciate what is now being discovered about the cosmos. The greater the appreciation of and wonder at the cosmos, the greater our appreciation of its Creator should be. John Haught suggests, "Science may be offering us, therefore, not less but more reason than ever for worship and gratitude."[7] It is my contention that the most influential and mind-expanding elements from the New Cosmology are the enhanced pictures from the Hubble Space Telescope. The actual images of distant nebulas, galaxies, and supernova explosions have transformed the imagination of humankind as has no other scientific discovery. While equivalent gains have been had at the subatomic level, we are reduced to taking the word of mathematicians and physicists or relying on the image of a mathematical equation since this reality is too small to visualize.

The Universe Story

It is now time to tell the New Universe Story. At this point in the twenty-first century, there is general scientific agreement that the universe as we know it began some 13.8 billion years ago and has been expanding outward since that time. The insights of three scientists who worked with Albert Einstein's theory of general relativity in the early twentieth century are particularly important and have led us to these conclusions. Dutch physicist Willem de Sitter wrote in 1917 that Einstein's theory of general relativity implied a changing, expanding cosmos rather than a static, fixed one as Einstein himself had theorized. Mathematician Alexander Friedmann also concluded in 1922 that the theory of general relativity was incompatible with a fixed universe. This led to Belgian priest and physicist George LeMaitre to theorize that the universe must have sprung from an infinitesimal physical speck.[8] In the late 1930s Russian-American physicist George Gamow expanded on this insight and theorized that the universe began with a fiery cosmic explosion. In a fraction of a second after there was nothing, space and time, mass, and energy

---

[7] Ibid., xiv.
[8] Ibid., 114.

expanded from an extremely compressed, hot, and dense state in an explosion of immense energy in what cosmologist Fred Hoyle would later name the "Big Bang." Swimme and Berry refer to it more elegantly as the primordial "Flaring Forth."[9] In 1965 scientists Robert Wilson and Arno Penzias from Bell Laboratories gave greater credence to the Big Bang theory when they discovered background microwave radiation that was consistent with an original explosion. All of these theories pressed scientists to search for the moment when the cosmos began. This conviction that the universe had a beginning overturned millennia of scientific consensus that the universe was infinite. In 1998–99 scientists led by Wendy Freedman and using data from the Hubble Space Telescope were able to calculate the accelerating expansion of the universe. From this data they were able to approximate the beginning of the universe at 13.7 billion years ago. As of March 2013, this estimate has increased to 13.8 billion years ago.

The story of the universe's development is informative and can be told in a series of eras that were characterized by a continuing lowering of temperature.[10] An initial explosion occurred of an infinitesimally small and unimaginatively dense element that contained all known matter, energy, space, and time. The explosion is judged to have been at more than 10^{32} degrees Kelvin, but plummeted to a mere million degrees in the first minute. While a minute might appear as a small amount of time, in the history of the universe, an immense amount of activity happened during this time. Within even the first second, scientists have discerned a number of eras. The "GUT Era" ("grand unification theories") was actually between 10^{-43} to 10^{-35} seconds, and the electromagnetic and the strong and weak nuclear forces were understood to be still unified with the gravitational force emerging separately. These four forces are the fundamental forces that govern matter. This era was followed by an outward expansion of space, energy, and matter during the time from 10^{-35} to 10^{-33} seconds. During this expansive period, scientist Paul Davies suggests that "the entire universe grew from one-thousand-millionth of the size of a proton to

---

[9] Swimme and Berry, *The Universe Story*, 17.

[10] I am basing my summary on Denis Edwards's narrative in *Creation, Humanity, Community: Building a New Theology* (Dublin: Gill and Macmillan Ltd., 1992), chap. 3.

several centimetres."[11] At the end of this "Inflation Era," the separation of the four forces mentioned above was complete ("Electroweak Era"). In the Quark Confinement Era between 10^{-6} and 2 seconds, "gluons of the strong nuclear force enabled quarks to coalesce into nuclear particles—protons, neutrons and their antiparticles."[12] At the end of the Inflation Era the universe released an enormous amount of energy in the form of radiation. In the extraordinary temperatures of the first second, this produced protons and particles that interacted in equilibrium. "Photons would decay into particles and antiparticles of matter, which would then annihilate one another, and form new photon pairs."[13] As the temperature decreased in the first second, however, there was an enormous loss of matter that might have resulted in the total collapse of the universe had not the ratio of matter to antimatter not been a billion and one particles of matter to a billion particles of antimatter. While this seemingly small residue of matter may not appear significant, in fact, the entire universe as we know it evolved from this matter.

The "Nucleosynthesis Era" was that period between one minute and five minutes after the Big Bang when the temperature reduced further to where nuclear reactions could occur. In this process hydrogen nuclei and helium nuclei formed out of the emerging plasma in the ratio of 25 percent helium to 75 percent hydrogen. After the first five minutes, the universe entered the "Radiation Era," which lasted a half-million years. As Denis Edwards says, at the end of this era, "matter and energy were uncoupled. And matter began to emerge as the dominant component of the expanding universe."[14] The "Era of Matter" lasted some ten billion years with the universe continuing to expand and cool, creating an expanding world of atoms, molecules, galaxies, and stars. Edwards notes, as the universe continued to expand, "slight unevenness in density meant there were locations where large clouds of hydrogen and helium accumulated" causing the be-

[11] Paul Davies, *Superforce: The Search for a Grand Unified Theory of Nature* (London: Unwin Paperbacks, 1985), 192.

[12] Edwards, *Creation*, 73, n. 27.

[13] Ibid., 35.

[14] Ibid., 37.

ginning of galaxies.[15] Under the influence of gravity, these pockets of gas began to collapse and heat up until nuclear fusion created more helium from hydrogen. Stars were formed. Continuing nuclear reactions "converted helium into the heavier elements, including the carbon, nitrogen, and oxygen from which we are made."[16] First generation stars exploded as supernovas, seeding their galaxies with heavier elements from which other stars and planets were formed. On one planet in a medium-sized galaxy, life emerged and some life forms became conscious beings. We are, Edwards notes, "the human community [that] springs from the fireball which carried within itself the potentiality for the universe which includes us and is unfolding around us."[17]

Earth's Story

The formation of Earth 4.6 billion years ago and its evolution is no less fascinating and awe inspiring than the evolution of the cosmos as a whole. In the Milky Way galaxy, "a supernova [star] exploded and a new star—our sun—emerged from the debris."[18] In addition, bands of gas circled the sun and planets were formed. The four inner planets (Mercury, Venus, Earth, and Mars) are rocky, while the others (Jupiter, Saturn, Uranus, and Neptune) are gaseous. The planets are held together by gravitational and radioactive elements. All activity on the three smallest planets (Mercury, Venus, and Mars) came to a stop with the formation of rocks, while the largest planets (Jupiter, Saturn, Uranus, and Neptune) continue in the gaseous state. As Cynthia Stokes Brown says, "Only Earth has a size that produces a gravitational and electromagnetic balance, which allows a solid rock crust to form around a burning core. Only Earth has a position in respect to the sun . . . that establishes a temperature range in which complex molecules can form."[19] Like the other planets and our moon,

[15] Denis Edwards, *How God Acts: Creation, Redemption, and Special Divine Action* (Minneapolis, MN: Fortress Press, 2010), 3.

[16] Ibid., 3.

[17] Edwards, *Creation*, 38.

[18] Cynthia Stokes Brown, *Big History: From the Big Bang to the Present* (New York: The New Press, 2007), 11.

[19] Ibid., 12.

Earth suffered collisions with meteors, asteroids, and planetoids during its first half-billion years. When it had cooled down sufficiently for a rock crust to form on its surface, lava rose up from its core, bringing chemicals forged in the interior to the surface. The atmosphere of methane, hydrogen, ammonia, and carbon was stirred by massive electrical storms. After another half-billion years, Earth was ready for living molecules to emerge.

While there is still some debate about the particulars of Charles Darwin's theory of evolution, there is widespread agreement on the idea of evolution itself, even as it is extended through the work of Gregor Mendel and later scientists in genetics. Thanks to the work of molecular biologists, we have come to appreciate that every living creature on Earth depends on the existence of the DNA molecule, which emerged between three and four billion years ago. We still do not know "how" inert matter developed into living organisms, but we know "that" it happened. From blue-green algae, the first living organisms, we can trace the development of human life. Two billion years ago sponges, algae, and fungi were the dominant forms of life on earth, while less than a billion years ago the first animal life appeared as marine invertebrates. Higher forms of plant life emerged 400 million years ago, while bony fish, rays, and sharks swam the ocean depths and fish-like amphibians took their first steps on dry land. In the Mezozoic Period (230–65 million years ago), reptiles dominated while mammals and birds emerged some 150 million years ago.

The story of human development requires some further explanation. According to astrophysicists, the atoms which make up our bodies had their origin in the nuclear reactions of the stars. In intense heat hydrogen was converted to helium, and the heavier elements were created and thrust out into space where they formed into galaxies, second- and third-generation stars (like our sun), and the planets. The very elements that make up the Earth and its human inhabitants were formed in the stars (except hydrogen, which came from the initial explosion). David Ellyard says it best:

> In this way was made all the iron we now find in our blood, all the phosphorus and calcium that strengthen our bones, all the sodium and potassium that drive signals along our nerves. Atoms so formed are thrown off into space by aged stars in their

death throes. Natural forces recycle them into new stars, into planets and plants and people. We are all made of stardust.[20]

From this development we can conclude that human beings are connected at the molecular level to everything else in the universe. While Ewert Cousins had argued that the second Axial Period was marked by a change from individual to global consciousness, the creation of a New Universe Story suggests that we are shifting even further into universe consciousness.

In what is called the *anthropic principle*, scientists tell us that had anything varied even the tiniest bit from the ways the universe actually unfolded, human life would not have evolved. Had the original dense particles of matter been just a bit larger, had the nuclear explosions been a bit hotter, had the rate of inflation been a bit faster or slower, had gravity, electromagnetism, the strong and weak nuclear forces been a bit different, etc., the universe would have collapsed in on itself or exploded outwardly too quickly before anything like galaxies and stars could have formed. But the universe did emerge as it did, and life formed and developed on Earth in the gradual way described above.

The Human Story

The gradual emergence of *Homo sapiens* from primates continues to be contested by some religious communities, but here too, there is general scientific agreement. The Cenozoic Period (65 million years ago) saw the appearance of the first primates. We have evidence of a creature which we call *Homo erectus* from about 2 million years ago, while modern humans emerged some 200,000 to 150,000 years ago. With the discovery of the DNA and RNA molecules by molecular biologists and biochemists, we have also learned that humans are related to every other living thing and that we share over 98 percent of our DNA with the higher primates. We can say with assurance that human beings are the cosmos come to consciousness. What we shall be in the future is still unknown, but if history has any lessons

---

[20] David Ellyard, *Sky Watch* (Crow's Nest, NSW, Australia: ABC Enterprises, 1988), 85, as quoted in Edwards, *Creation*, 41.

to teach us, we should not be surprised that change and development will continue to occur.

In an effort to make clear how late humankind is in the evolutionary process, John Haught has worked out a schema for the various stages of evolution that is illuminating.[21] He suggests that we consider having a thirty-volume set of books of 450 pages in each with each page representing one million years. The Big Bang would be in volume one, page one, but the first 21 volumes would show no signs of life at all. Earth's story begins in volume 21, but life doesn't appear until volume 22. The Cambrian Period with its explosion of life forms does not show up until volume 29. Dinosaurs come in around the middle of volume 30; only during the last sixty-five pages of volume 30 does mammalian life flourish, while our hominid ancestors appear only at several pages from the end of volume 30. Modern humans only show up at the bottom of the final page. As Haught sums up, "The entire history of human intelligence, ethics, religious aspiration, and scientific discovery takes up only the last few lines on the last page of the last volume."[22] Clearly, the history of humankind makes its appearance quite late in the development of the known universe.

While scientific discoveries at the macro level have occupied my presentation of the New Universe Story until now, the developments of science at the atomic and subatomic levels have likewise brought us into heretofore uncharted territory. Through advances in mathematics, mechanics, and astronomy, Western science had come to trust that its knowledge of the governing laws of the universe led to a certitude in the perception of what science could provide regarding predictability (the so-called Newtonian universe). In addition, science had deduced that by breaking down elements of the universe to their constitutive parts, it could fully understand these realities. This led to a mechanistic view of the world and the sense that it was deterministic and predictable. More recent studies at the atomic and subatomic levels quickly challenged those positions. Quantum mechanics, for example, has changed our notion that the smallest building blocks of reality are separate objects. Rather, it suggests that interrelationships are fundamental to the universe. It has also shown, according

---

[21] Haught, *Christianity and Science*, xii.
[22] Ibid., xii.

to biochemist Arthur Peacocke, "that there is indeterminacy in the measurement of certain quantities in quantum mechanical systems."[23] Probability and uncertainty have replaced predictability and determinism. "We cannot achieve unlimited predictability," Peacocke argues, "because of our inability ever to determine the initial conditions with sufficient precision, in spite of the deterministic character of Newton's laws."[24]

Other discoveries of quantum physics are also important to our understanding of reality. One such discovery is that matter is actually a manifestation of energy. Light, which previously had been understood as a wave, was discovered to exhibit properties called photons, or little quanta of energy. In other words, light was found to behave as a wave or a particular. German physicist Werner Heisenberg discovered that uncertainty is part of the dynamic nature of particles. He claimed this because the more precisely the position of a particle is determined, the less precisely the momentum is known. This has become known as the "uncertainty principle." It has helped us to understand that observation determines reality; there is no clear line between subject and object. We are all subjects in an interrelated universe.

Biologists have also helped us understand that "matter is not composed of basic building blocks but rather of complicated webs of relations in which the observer constitutes a final link in the chain of observational processes, and the properties of any atomic object can be understood only in terms of interaction between object and observer."[25] This sense of the relatedness of all reality has led to the development of systems thinking. Ludwig von Bertalanffy, the founder of systems thinking in the 1920s, wrote "Whereas Newtonian mechanics was a science of forces and trajectories, evolutionary thinking—thinking in terms of change, growth and development, required a new science of complexity."[26]

---

[23] Arthur Peacocke, *Paths from Science towards God: The End of All Our Exploring* (Oxford, UK: Oneworld, 2001), 97.

[24] Ibid.

[25] Ilia Delio, *The Emergent Christ: Exploring the Meaning of Catholic in an Evolutionary Universe* (Maryknoll, NY: Orbis Books, 2011), 25.

[26] As cited in Fritjof Capra, *The Web of Life: A New Scientific Understanding of Living Systems* (New York: Doubleday, 1996), 47.

Chaos theory, developed in the 1960s, worked with the relationship of data in open systems. It was discovered that small changes in initial conditions can cause large changes in long-term results (the so-called butterfly effect). As described by Ilia Delio, chaos theory has three main points: *sensitivity to initial conditions* (small disturbances of the current trajectory may lead to significantly different future behaviors); *strange attractors* (basins of attraction within a system can lure the system into new patterns of order over time); and *fractals* (geometric shapes formed from repeated patterns of behavior at different scales).[27] This has led us to understand that the universe is not related simply as cause and effect or like a machine; rather, networks of relationships characterize our world and our lives. We are, in effect, part of a web of life that is interconnected and interdependent at every level.

While this knowledge of the relationality of things comes at the quantum level, it is instructive on the ecological level as well. While humankind in the first Axial Period had related to the natural world as objects to be used for human purposes, we are now seeing that it is essential to view and honor the interrelationship of all creation. In other words, we are recognizing that the inert "stuff" of the earth and all other living plants and creatures are tied in a web of relationships that cannot be ignored. Our own ecological crisis should force us to rethink our relationship with the world and change our living habits to allow the flourishing of all—air, land, sea, plants, animals, and humans alike. There are those who argue that we are on the verge of the sixth major extinction that Earth has known, and it is being caused by human beings. Only concerted human effort at the global level will enable us to avert such a tragedy.

In conclusion, we can say the New Science of the last 150 years has taught us more about the universe than all human knowledge had amassed prior to this period combined. While clearly major questions remain (What was there before the Big Bang? What started the Big Bang? Are there other universes besides our own? etc.), we have developed theories on the emergence of the known universe, on the relationship of energy, matter, time, and space, and on life's emergence from inert elements and mind from matter. Importantly, we

---

[27] Delio, *Emergent Christ*, 26.

have traced human relationship with all other living and nonliving things, even back to the elements of the stars themselves. Our story, the human story, can only be told from this point on within the story of the universe. The Universe Story is our story.

Part II

Assessing Theology in Light of Contemporary Science

In part 1 of this book, I suggested that the only responsible relationship between religion and science is that of *contact/ conversation* and *confirmation* (using John Haught's taxonomy). *Conflict* pits science and religion against one another as if they were both answering the same set of questions and fails to distinguish the two. *Contrast* respects that science and religion are asking radically different questions and, thus, conflict between the two is impossible. The contrast approach typically separates science's question about *how* things exist and theology's quest for understanding *why* they exist. *Conflation* fails to distinguish the particular focus and methods of each field, and collapses one into the other. While *contrast* is a step beyond *conflict* and *conflation*, it fails to take into account the contribution that one could make to the other. This would seem to be a lost opportunity, especially if we admit that both science and religion are interested in truth, albeit by different means.

Part 2 of this book aims to synthesize different theological positions on some of the major issues of systematic theology —creation, God/Trinity, Christology, and Pneumatology—by those theologians who have taken the New Cosmology seriously as an important conversation partner (*contact* and *confirmation*). At this stage, systematic theology has made initial steps in this direction, and I have chosen to include two or three theologians who have contributed to the conversation on any given topic.

▍ Chapter 3 ▍

Creation Theology, God, and the Big Bang

A Theology of Creation

The Catholic view of creation has its roots in the biblical witness, both Old and New Testaments. While recognizing that the Bible could be read in a literal or a theological way, a contemporary reading suggests that the Bible should be interpreted as a theological text, exploring the nature of God and creation from the perspective of an elect people—Israel or the church. The doctrine of creation has traditionally been comprised of three dimensions: *creatio ex nihilo, creatio continua*, and *creatio nova*. (We will explore these three dimensions in a little more detail below.) A further extension of creation theology would also insist that humankind is made in the image and likeness of God (*imago Dei*), and that creation is not necessary but rather contingent. That is, creation is a free act of a loving God who empties self out in order to create something different from God's self, and that creation depends on God for its existence and fulfillment.

A central tenet of the doctrine of creation is that God created the world out of nothing (*creatio ex nihilo*). This truth has been held since biblical times, but its reiteration has always been in response to new cultural contexts and new challenges. That is, it has been defended against positions as diverse as creation accounts in the Near East that argued for a polytheistic account of creation; Greek philosophical accounts on the eternal nature of the universe; Manichean and Gnostic beliefs in a dual source of creation and a duality of matter and spirit; the theory of evolution, scientific materialism, and more be-sides. The principal aim of the doctrine *creatio ex nihilo* is to maintain the absolute transcendence of God over creation. It also includes the teaching that the God of Judeo-Christian faith is the only God, and it is this God who is ground and source for all that exists.

The doctrine of creation also includes the belief in God's continuing creation (*creatio continua*), which countered the deist notion of a God who created at the beginning of time and then allowed creation to develop on its own with no further intervention. The *creatio continua* teaching holds that God continues to create at every moment of the universe's existence. A third dimension of God's creative activity which has not received as much attention as it deserves is that of *creatio nova* or that God is the author of the new creation at the full-ness of time.

It is now time to look at two contemporary theological views on creation that take the current cosmology into account.

John Haught on Creation

It is Haught's conviction that theology and science are distinct fields in terms of method and content, and can be considered help-fully under the rubric of *contrast*.[1] The scientific approach acknowl-edges that a consensus has been reached by all cosmologists that creation had a definite beginning. This consensus did away with the previously accepted position that the universe was eternal. (This position would seem to support the theological doctrine of creation by God, but Haught argues that this is not entirely true, since even an eternal universe could still be a created one.) Even with the ac-knowledgment of creation's beginning, scientists are increasingly content with the belief (scientism) that the universe is so vast that it can be its own foundation for life and thought. This belief in natural-ism does not need a doctrine of creation by the divine.

While acknowledging the insights of contemporary science, a *con-trast* approach holds that religion is about something entirely different

---

[1] This summary is taken mainly from John Haught, *Christianity and Science: Toward a Theology of Nature* (Maryknoll, NY: Orbis Books, 2007), chap. 7; and *Science and Reli-gion: From Conflict to Conversation* (Mahwah, NJ: Paulist Press, 1995), chap. 5.

from astrophysics, and therefore the doctrine of creation is neither undermined nor affirmed by Big Bang science. Creation is not so much an account about origins as it is about the answer to the question "Why is there something rather than nothing?"[2] In the *contrast* approach, only theology has a response to those questions of intent, meaning, and purpose. Despite current science, the Christian doctrine of creation still stands on its own and has its own consequences. Haught argues that the realization of God's gracious act of self-giving to creation and to the human community in particular should engender gratitude and praise. In fact, many biblical texts do exactly that (see, for example, Psalms 8, 19, 29, 33, 104 among many other psalms), and these texts are used in Christian liturgy in thanksgiving and praise for God's creation. At this point science and theology are content to stand side by side, answering different questions.

While there is clearly something attractive and safe about leaving theology and science in their separate realms, there is more to be gained in the interaction between science and theology than just *contrast*. Haught finds *contact* to be a very fruitful activity for both science and theology. One of the first and most important contributions of the New Cosmology to theology is that it has brought the universe back into central focus. Since the turn to the subject of Emmanuel Kant, theology has become exceedingly anthropocentric. While there were many gains in this endeavor, nonetheless, the universe was left merely as the backdrop for human being and action. It may legitimately be asked if our current ecological crisis stems in some part from the disconnection between theology and the cosmos dating back to the Reformation. The turn back to the cosmos situates the human person in a much larger context, and raises the provocative point that perhaps the human species is not the sole reason for the universe's existence. While this overturns the emphasis on humanity in recent theology and thus may be disturbing, nonetheless, theology needs to explore this possibility. In other words, Big Bang science has thrown the question of why the universe exists back to theology to be addressed in a new context. In the meantime we can continue to be grateful for the fact that we are a blessed part of this

<hr>

[2] Haught, *Christianity and Science*, 110.

great cosmic adventure.[3] In fact Big Bang science can contribute to humanity's awe at the sheer wonder of creation, something that holds an important place in religious practice.[4]

The second contribution that the New Cosmology makes to theological reflection is the discovery that the universe is still developing. This presents theology with another opportunity to consider *creatio continua* or the continuing nature of God's creative activity. In addition, Haught argues that the fact that the universe is evolving around us and in us gives fresh support to Christianity's belief that a New Creation (*creatio nova*) is still ahead of us. Rather than only being preoccupied with the past, science has also turned its attention to the future, asking the question "Where are we going?" Here Haught finds the clearest contribution of one field to the other. The Judeo-Christian belief in a God of promise who opens up a new future for the world is supported by the scientific view of the still unfolding nature of the cosmos. Here is where the ultimate intelligibility of the cosmos resides: not only in looking at the past, but looking toward the future.[5]

God's decision to create something other than God's self in love means that the universe has not only been created at a given point in time, it has also been created with a kind of autonomy. This is not the deism of the nineteenth century, but an acknowledgment that God's self-emptying love truly "must will the independence of creation."[6] We have learned from science that differentiation is also a dimension of the cosmos, as is the tendency to organize and relate. Here theology can rejoice with science that ultimate unity in differentiation is the goal of the universe.

In addition to theology's gains from science, Haught argues that science too is finding itself asking some of the "why" questions that have previously been the purview of theology. Reflecting a return to the cosmos, science is asking not only why we are here, but "why the universe is here and why it is able to give rise to life, mind, and persons."[7] Science has come to share religion's enthusiasm for questions

---

[3] Haught, *Science and Religion*, 110.
[4] Ibid., 116.
[5] Ibid., 117–18.
[6] Haught, *Christianity and Science*, 129.
[7] Ibid., 127.

of origins and meaning. Without conflating one into the other, Haught suggests that science shares with religion "the ineradicably mythic orientation of human consciousness."[8] We are both concerned about our roots.

Regarding the role of theology in *confirming* the scientific enterprise, Haught argues that theology's belief that creation is not necessary and is contingent supports the scientific endeavor of discovery. If the world was exactly as it had to be given existing laws, science would have no other function than to deduce the universe's properties from those laws. The very contingency of the universe and the fact of emergence suggests that science has to continually engage in inductive and empirical research. Creation theology supports "the inductive method of natural science that always makes room for endless new fields of research."[9]

In summary, Haught has carried the science/religion conversation into the area of creation theology. While science maintains that the cosmos is its own cause, theology stands firm in its position that God is the source, sustaining power, and goal of the cosmos. The *contrast* between these two positions is obvious. But Haught also argues that science's discoveries provide rich material for theological reflection on creation. He suggests that the New Science of the last 150 years has placed the universe back into central focus for theological reflection. This turn to the cosmos suggests that theologians take an interest in the cosmos for its own sake and not just as a background for human concerns. Big Bang science also encourages awe in response to the magnificence of creation, engendering praise and thanksgiving in believers. Another result of the science and theology dialogue is the interest in a still-developing cosmos and in a God who opens up a new future for the cosmos, one of unity in differentiation. On the other hand, theology contributes to science's renewed interest in questions of intent and purpose. Lastly, theology confirms the scientific enterprise by suggesting that the contingent nature of the universe supports the scientific endeavor of discovery.

---

[8] Haught, *Science and Religion*, 118.
[9] Haught, *Christianity and Science*, 132.

Denis Edwards on Creation

It would be fair to characterize Australian theologian Denis Edwards's work under the category of *contact*, although he is not as methodical in his approach as is Haught. The presumption that underlies Edwards's projects in general is that theology must be in dialogue with the New Science if it is to remain viable for our age.

Edwards begins his treatment of creation and the New Science with the admonition that even with a theology of creation, we must begin with the revelation of God in Jesus Christ. It is in the Christ event that we know of God: "God is revealed as self-giving love."[10] In addition, we find that a theology of God and a theology of creation are inexorably entwined. From this foundation Edwards goes on to argue five points regarding creation: that God's self-bestowing love enables emergence; it works through chance and lawfulness; it supports creaturely autonomy; it accepts the limits of creaturely processes; and it acts in a noninterventionist way.

Working with Karl Rahner's theology of evolution, Edwards begins with the specificity and historical character of God's Divine Acts. He suggests that creation is an act of God's self-bestowal. "God chooses to give God's self in love to what is not divine, and so creation comes to be."[11] This implies, first of all, that creation, the incarnation, and redemption are all within God's one act of self-bestowing love. In other words, it is according to the being of God that these acts are one; the specificity of grace is in God's relating in differentiated ways to all created beings and processes. Secondly, with Duns Scotus and Karl Rahner, Edwards subscribes to the idea that the incarnation was intended from the beginning of creation. The Christ was not sent as a remedy for sin; although with the reality of sin, the incarnation is a radical act of forgiveness, healing, and liberation. In addition, Edwards says, "God's self-giving in the incarnation is the very purpose and meaning of creation."[12] This implies that the scientific facts of evolution are part of a larger story of God's purpose in creation, redemption, and fulfillment. God's self-donation to the world is a permanent

---

[10] This summary of Edwards's theology of creation is taken mainly from Denis Edwards, *How God Acts: Creation, Redemption, and Special Divine Action* (Minneapolis, MN: Fortress Press, 2010), 35.

[11] Ibid., 39.

[12] Ibid., 40.

commitment of God's self to the world. In Jesus, God commits God's self to the world, and thus partakes in the very evolutionary, material world for all eternity. Creation is directed from within, Edwards says, toward God's self-bestowal. God is not interested simply in creating something other than God's self; God is interested in creating, sustaining, and fulfilling creation through God's own gift of self. In this sense, "the universe emerges, and life evolves on Earth, in the process of God's self-bestowal."[13]

While this act of self-bestowal can be understood from God's perspective, it is also possible to look at the action from the perspective of creation. In Edwards's understanding, the effect of God's immanent presence is the creaturely capacity for self-transcendence. In other words, "there is an evolutionary dynamism that is truly intrinsic to creation but occurs through the creative power of the immanent God."[14] This is true for all dimensions of creation including human beings. The universe emerges into self-conscious, free beings, capable of response to God's freely given grace. This has implications for our understanding of Christology. "Jesus Christ," Edwards suggests, "is the radical self-transcendence of the created universe into God."[15] Like Rahner, Edwards argues that in Jesus the self-bestowal of God occurs and creation's acceptance of that self-bestowal takes place in a historically definitive way.

Science has led to previously unimagined insight into creation's processes, emergent qualities, and open-ended potentialities. From a theological perspective, God's self-bestowal does nothing to limit creation's autonomy, but paradoxically increases it. God enables the universe to run by its own laws and processes that are integral to it. God always respects the independence and integrity of what God has created. This puts God at risk in this process, Edwards suggests, because God's creative act allows creation to run by its own laws and chance. But this also implies that God "feels with each of them a transcendent capacity for empathy, sharing their joys and their sufferings with unthinkable and vulnerable divine love."[16] God's freedom is to be understood as a limited kind of freedom that accepts

[13] Ibid., 43.
[14] Ibid., 44.
[15] Ibid.
[16] Ibid., 49.

creation as it is; God works within the limits that are intrinsic to created reality. This does not mean that God is less than omnipotent, but rather that God is acting out of God's own nature: a radical self-giving love. This love "has an unimaginable capacity to respect the autonomy and independence of creatures, to work with them patiently, and to bring all things to fulfillment."[17] This understanding of God's creative act is absolutely compatible with an emerging and increasingly complex universe. Rather than imaging God as the grand clockmaker of deism, Edwards images God as an artist "exploring in creation, responding in spontaneity and freedom to what is given."[18]

In summary, Edwards's theology of creation is grounded in Christ Jesus who reveals a God of self-donation in creating other reality and sustaining it in existence and in fulfillment. Sin is not the reason for the incarnation; it is God's unfathomable love that intended the incarnation from all time. Jesus Christ is the historic instance of God's self-bestowal and the human response to that bestowal. That love of self-donation, in a sense, limits God's power in that God not only intends but actually enhances creation's capacity of autonomy and freedom. There is an inner dynamism to creation that emerges into life and mind, a transcendence to the more. God works with creation as it is, which includes processes of order, law, and chance. This implies a noninterventionist God; God's action is constantly present and interior to an emergent universe and works through the laws of nature rather than violating or suspending them.

A Theology of God and the New Science

Writing a theology of God is a complex task in that any theology of God in the Christian dispensation must take into account the self-disclosure of God in Jesus Christ, the role of the Spirit, the Trinity, the themes of revelation and redemption, among the other themes of systematic theology. Christianity's God cannot be understood without the recognition that we come to know God primarily through the revelation of God in Christ and the Spirit, through scripture and in tradition. While for many centuries it was traditional to explore a

---

[17] Ibid., 51.
[18] Ibid., 54.

general doctrine of "God" (*De Deo uno*) and then of the "Trinity" (*De Deo trino*), and to consider God *ad intra* and God *ad extra*, more current theology finds these separations flawed and distorted.[19] In the summaries that follow, these traditional categories are avoided in an effort to articulate a more integrated theology of God.

Regarding the interface of a theology of God and Christology, Christians experience and understand the God of love first through their experience and understanding of Jesus Christ in the power of the Spirit. Through this reading of the tradition, Christians come to know a God who can be understood only as utterly personal, self-disclosing, and self-emptying. In addition, humanity also knows of God through reflection on its own desire for self-transcendence, truth, and love. From our own experience of self, we can come to know the one who is ground of our subjectivity, relationality, self-possession, and autonomy. Yet knowledge of God is not to be limited to an anthropocentric knowledge either. Scripture tells us of God's being as creator and sustainer of the universe, initiator of the covenant, and hope for salvation and fulfillment.

Classical theology has struggled to name God using the criteria of appropriateness for the identity of God and intelligibility for attributes of God. Catholic theology has always opted for an analogical naming of the God who, even after our best efforts at naming, remains mystery. In classical theism, God has often been described in metaphysical qualities (under the influence of Greek thought). God is (against atheism); God is one (against polytheism); God is transcendent over creation (against pantheism). In addition, God is understood as the origin, sustainer, and end-of-all reality. In some forms of theism, God is understood not only as transcendent over creation but separated from it as well, thereby raising the question of God and suffering. Due to a dependence on a metaphysical notion of perfection and an understanding of God as pure act, God was never associated with suffering, since suffering implied subjection to another. Since God was not dependent on any other, suffering in God was deemed impossible. This *apathic* God or a God without pathos

[19] See David Tracy, "Approaching the Christian Understanding of God," in *Systematic Theology: Roman Catholic Perspectives*, vol. 1, ed. Francis Schüssler Fiorenza and John P. Galvin (Minneapolis, MN: Fortress Press, 1991), 133ff.

or suffering tries to preserve God from finitude. However, the pervasiveness of suffering led people to question God's love and God's apparent intention not to intervene in nature or the human community to stem that suffering.

If God wills only the good, then why does God allow suffering? This painful question raises issues of whether God suffers, but also whether God is omnipotent. Could it be that God is not able to intervene and relieve suffering? Must it be that God allows suffering to happen for some good purpose? In the face of horrific suffering, what could that purpose be? Recent liberation theologians of all stripes are challenging this notion of an apathic God in the face of radical suffering. As theologian Elizabeth Johnson notes, "the idea of the impassible, omnipotent God appears riddled with inadequacies. The idea of God simply cannot remain unaffected by the basic datum of so much suffering and death."[20]

It remains to be seen what effect the New Universe Story will have on our theology of God, especially regarding the questions of cosmic suffering, apparent extravagant waste, and the mystery of death.

Arthur Peacocke on God

Physical biochemist and theologian Arthur Peacocke is also of the opinion that advances in science in the last 150 years are the greatest challenge (and perhaps threat) to received monotheistic beliefs about God, nature, and humanity.[21] His purpose in writing is to show that "the scientific vista for the third millennium, or at least the twenty-first century, constitutes a stimulus to theology to become more encompassing and inclusive, but only if theology radically alters its widely assumed paradigms."[22] Unless theology, he argues, takes into account the New Universe Story, it will be moribund and doomed. His task, like that of Haught, is to look at the changes to theology that result from a conversation (*contact*) with science, particularly regarding a theology of God. Certainly no arguments from science can "prove"

---

[20] Elizabeth Johnson, *She Who Is: The Mystery of God in Feminist Theological Discourse* (New York: Crossroad, 1992), 249.

[21] Arthur Peacocke, *Paths from Science towards God: The End of All Our Exploring* (Oxford, UK: Oneworld Publications, 2001), 65.

[22] Ibid., 66.

God's existence or character, as these are clearly in the realm of theology and faith. However, the insights into the workings of the universe by the plethora of scientific fields that have gone into the writing of the New Universe Story do suggest to theologians that a classical theology of God needs further development.

Peacocke begins his observations by stating that if creation is as it is and as science tells us it is, then we can learn something of the nature of the Creator. We have learned in great detail that creation is at once rich and has a variety of entities, structures, and processes. It is diverse, fecund, and has multiple levels of complexity. If this is so, then the Creator must be of such kind that it has the capacity to give existence to this variety of entities, structures, and processes. God must be, Peacocke argues, some kind of "diversity-in-unity, one Being of unfathomable richness, capable of multiple expressions and variegated outreach."[23] Since the world is rational and intelligible, then the Creator must be "supremely and unsurpassedly rational."[24] It must be further omniscient and omnipotent in order to give all-that-is the possibility of knowledge and power. If all-that-is is made up of matter-energy-space-time, then its Creator must be omnipresent and eternal. If the universe has become conscious and self-conscious in the human person, then the Creator must be at least personal or supra-personal.[25]

We are also learning from science that the world is in evolution through law and chance or randomness. This raises the question of how God relates to these two necessities. Here Peacocke argues that for the theist, God the Creator is "unfolding the divinely endowed potentialities of the universe through a process in which its creative possibilities and propensities become actualized."[26] Using a musical metaphor, Peacocke suggests that God works much like the great improviser J. S. Bach, who starts with a simple melody and weaves complex harmonies and structures out of it. Peacocke calls this God who unfolds the potentialities of the universe "the Improvisor of unsurpassed ingenuity."[27]

[23] Ibid., 40.
[24] Ibid., 41.
[25] Ibid., 42.
[26] Ibid., 77.
[27] Ibid., 79.

Further, Peacocke argues, if God creates all-that-is in its complexity
and diversity, then God must intend it thus and take something like
joy and delight in creation.[28] In a sense, the turn to the cosmos suggests that all reality has value unto itself and exists not only for the
purposes of humanity, who has arrived quite late on the scene of
cosmic evolution, but for its own purpose. Peacocke suggests that
the Creator of all-that-is is of such kind to be a God who desires the
existence of other beings and desires to share ultimate reality with
this creation.

Our growing knowledge of an evolutionary cosmos complete with
its explosive propensities and upheavals on a massive scale presses
the theist to ask why there is such pain, predation, suffering, and
death in the evolutionary process and what this says about the
Creator of such a world. Responding to the question of suffering and
the tradition of an *apathic* God, Peacocke proposes that *"God suffers
in, with and under the creative processes of the world* with their costly
unfolding in time."[29] Positing suffering in God leads Peacocke to
reframe the relationship between God and creation and to recast a
theology of God that allows for suffering within God without loss of
God's omnipotence or being.

The world exists in some sense "in God," and God identifies, participates, and suffers with this world. This is a pan*en*theistic account
that states that all is in God and God is in all, although God is not to
be identified with created reality and is always more than creation.
Christian theology has attributed some self-limitation in God by the
very fact that God has created something other than God's self and
given it a degree of autonomy. Now, through the lens of cosmic and
biological evolution, we can conclude that this self-limitation involves
costly suffering to God. This is not a sign of imperfection in God as
Greek philosophy would suggest; it is a sign of the self-emptying of
God who has always been understood in the Judeo-Christian tradition as a God of unrelenting love. God takes such risks as creating
free human persons for the ultimate purpose of having the joy of
sharing divine life with them, if they should so choose. A consequence
of that intention, however, involves the possibility of much degrada-

[28] Ibid., 85.
[29] Ibid., 86; italics in the original.

tion and evil. As Peacocke suggests, this results in a "continuing self-limitation and self-emptying vulnerability of God to the very processes God creates in order to achieve an overriding purpose, the emergence of free persons."[30] Peacocke further suggests that in this model, female metaphors are more applicable to the understanding of Ultimate Reality and give new meaning to Paul's poetic vision of the whole creation as "groaning in labor pains" in Romans 8.[31]

While a classical theology of God has clearly noted that the God of Jews, Christians, and Moslems is both a God of immanence and a God of transcendence, science is pressing the question of both. Peacocke suggests that the realization of the universe as a dynamic, unfolding event through complex processes and systems of systems asks theologians to rethink what immanence and transcendence mean and reaffirm their importance. In his terms, "the processes revealed by the sciences are in themselves God acting as Creator, and God is not to be found as some kind of additional influence or factor added on to the processes of the world God is creating."[32] Unlike the classical theistic model that posits "substance" to God and that there is a space outside of God where the created is located, the panentheistic model again enables the theologian to say that God's infinity encloses all finite beings, and that there is no place "outside God" for anything that could exist. "God creates all-that-is *within* Godself."[33] In addition, God incorporates all individual systems and systems of systems within God's self. The suffering of the natural world is experienced by God as within God's own self, and so God experiences its sufferings directly, not from the outside. In the panentheistic model and with the discoveries of the New Science, we are able to honor both the transcendence of God beyond creation and the immanence of God in all things and processes, although we do have to revise our theology of an *apathic* God.

In summary, Peacocke argues that we can learn much of the Creator by science's exploration of the universe's entities, structures, and processes. The God of a diverse, fecund, and complex universe is one

[30] Ibid., 89.
[31] Ibid., 87.
[32] Ibid., 138.
[33] Ibid., 139.

of "diversity-in-unity," a Being of unfathomable richness, rational and intelligent, omniscient and omnipotent, and at least personal. This God works through the laws of nature and randomness which God has created, and explores creation's potentialities like a great musical improviser. This is a God who delights in creation and who suffers in, with, and under the creative processes of the world. Peacocke's is a pan*en*theistic account which states that all is in God although God is not to be identified or limited to creation. God is self-limiting in that God has chosen to create an "other," particularly a free human person, and that God is a God of unrelenting love. Peacocke argues for abandoning "substance" notions for God which leave creation "outside" God in favor of an approach that includes all in God's own self, even while maintaining God's transcendence and immanence.

Denis Edwards on God

Theologian Denis Edwards writes from the perspective that intellectual integrity demands that Christian theology take into account the broad lines of evolutionary development with its dynamic of natural selection and chance. His question is, "How can we talk meaningfully of the Christian God in an evolutionary world?"[34] Edwards's response is that we can build on our biblical foundations as well as our theological foundations, the latter as diverse as Richard of St. Victor, Bonaventure, Teilhard de Chardin, and Karl Rahner, among others.

Edwards submits that a theology of God that takes evolution seriously is a "Trinitarian vision of God as a God of mutual relations, a God who is communion in love, a God who is friendship beyond all comprehension."[35] He grounds this understanding particularly in the Gospel of John, which works with the Greek term *menein en* or "abiding in" to explain the relationship of the Father, the Son, and the Spirit and all Christian believers. Repeatedly John uses this term

---

[34] This summary of Edwards's thought on a theology of God is taken mainly from Denis Edwards, *The God of Evolution: A Trinitarian Theology* (Mahwah, NJ: Paulist Press, 1999), 3.

[35] Ibid., 15.

to describe how the Spirit descends and abides in Jesus (1:32-34); how the Father abides in Jesus (14:10-11); how the Spirit will abide with the disciples (14:15-17); how Jesus abides in the disciples and they in him (14:18-20). Edwards argues that in John's gospel we have a developed understanding of the dynamic relationship of mutual indwelling between the members of the Trinity and them with the disciples.

Edwards uses as his conversation partner Richard of St. Victor, who stresses the friendship that characterizes trinitarian relations. Richard points to the sense of *koinonia* or communion and *perichoresis* or being-in-another that marks Divine friendship. This friendship does not just include God simply loving God's self; it extends to another. The friendship which characterizes the Father and Son breaks out beyond the two to include a third—the Spirit. Edwards argues that this kind of mutual friendship "is the fundamental principle from which all creatures spring."[36] This relational view of God corresponds to the evolutionary sciences which are learning of the interrelationship and interdependence of all things in the universe. If all creatures can be understood in these same terms, beings-in-relation, then so too can God be called Persons-in-Relation, the Creator of such a world.

Edwards then explores how the universe and God as Persons-in-Relation are interconnected. Like Peacocke, Edwards rejects the idea that God can be understood as being in a "place" next to creation or that God reaches "out" into the world at particular moments. He suggests as an alternative view that God is present and active everywhere, even as God transcends all of creation. "The universe," he says, "can be understood as unfolding 'within' the Trinitarian relations of mutual love."[37] All of creation—original and ongoing—takes place within God. Referencing Bonaventure, Edwards sees creation as "the free ecstatic overflow of the fecundity of the divine Trinitarian love."[38] Edwards, like Peacocke, wants to move to a pan*en*theistic approach that situates all beings in God and God in all being (without identifying God with creation). God is immanent to every creature, luring them into being and holding them in being. Relating this

[36] Ibid., 24.
[37] Ibid., 30.
[38] Ibid., 31.

understanding of God to the evolutionary sciences, Edwards argues that "[E]volution takes place in God."[39]

The God of the universe is also a God who self-limits so as not to overwhelm creation. In this sense, God is not to be understood as radically omnipotent. Rather, God, as revealed in Jesus Christ, is vulnerable. Omnipotence must be understood as the power to give one's self freely in love. This is the wisdom of God of which Paul speaks. Using a theology of *kenosis* or pouring out, Edwards wants to acknowledge that this is a way of understanding God's suffering with creation, but only if we keep in balance God's desire to bring healing and salvation. God self-limits by allowing creation to be exactly as it is, and God "suffers" the consequences of human free-dom and the limitations of natural laws and chance. On this issue, Edwards helpfully quotes Walter Kasper. I include the whole com-ment here for its ability to tie together these seeming "contraries" in God:

> For the Bible, then, the revelation of God's omnipotence and the revelation of God's love are not contraries. God need not strip himself of his omnipotence to reveal his love. On the contrary, it requires omnipotence to be able to surrender oneself and give oneself away; and it requires omnipotence to be able to take oneself back in the giving and to preserve the independence and freedom of the recipient. Only an almighty love can give itself wholly to the other and be a helpless love.[40]

Edwards is anxious to maintain that this understanding of a God who suffers with creation must be kept in dialogue with a tradition that also holds God as unchanging (immutable), all powerful (omni-potent), and transcendent. God is unchanging in love and faithful to divine promises. God does not suffer as a sign of limit; the God we know in the revelation of Jesus Christ is a God who is self-emptying. This is a revelation of true divinity. God is also all-powerful in the sense of bringing all of creation to its fulfillment. Finally, God is said to suffer with the universe while always remaining transcendent.

[39] Ibid., 34.

[40] Walter Kasper, *The God of Jesus Christ* (Malden, MA: Blackwell, 2000), 195, as quoted in Denis Edwards, *How God Acts: Creation, Redemption, and Special Divine Action* (Minneapolis, MN: Fortress Press, 2010), 31.

God is never a creature among other creatures; God alone is Creator. Edwards helpfully reminds us that all these efforts to name the unnameable are by way of analogy, meaning that God transcends even our best efforts at naming.[41]

In summary, Edwards argues that a theology of God which takes evolution into account must be a trinitarian theology of mutual relations. God's identity is one of unsurpassable friendship and communion. This view of God as relation fits in well with science's own discoveries of the relational nature of the universe at all levels. Edwards subscribes to a pan*en*theistic view, which holds that all exists within the trinitarian relations of mutual love, without ever identifying God with creation. For Edwards, God self-limits, and is revealed as a kenotic God who pours self out in infinite love. God suffers with creation at all levels while remaining immutable, omnipotent, and transcendent.

John Haught on God

Haught wishes to replace theological ideas about God that are not up to the task of meeting the challenges of the New Science, particularly Darwinism or neo-Darwinism (Darwin's theory of evolution plus genetics).[42] Christianity, as he sees it, has shaped a theology of God that is too associated with order, thereby needing to connect disorder or chaos with the demonic. The result is that our theology of God is not able to meet the challenge of evolutionary science with its apparent randomness, blind experimentation, and impersonality. Quoting David Hull, Haught says that such an approach does not take into account an evolutionary process that is "rife with happenstance, contingency, incredible waste, death, pain and horror," leaving a God who must be "careless, indifferent, almost diabolical."[43] But what, Haught asks, if God is not only the God of order, but disturbing wellspring of novelty; what if the cosmos is still an unfinished process? This understanding of God fits better with the unfolding knowledge of science. In fact, not only is theology not threatened by

---

[41] Edwards, *How God Acts*, 30–31

[42] This summary of Haught's thought on God is taken mainly from John Haught, *God after Darwin: A Theory of Evolution*, 2nd ed. (Boulder, CO: Westview Press, 2008).

[43] Haught, *God after Darwin*, 6.

science's discoveries—these discoveries are in fact a gift to theology. I will now summarize Haught's insights into what an adequate theology of God would look like if it responded to the challenges of neo-Darwinism.

Haught insists that we must distance ourselves from thoughts of God as put forth in "Intelligent Design." This is a set of ideas that seeks to curb the influence of Darwinism by arguing that speciation and cellular complexity are too sophisticated to have come from a gradual evolution, but need an intelligent designer.[44] What is objectionable in this position is that it wants to maintain God as the intelligent designer as a scientific fact, something that scientists clearly oppose. This pits religion against science, and conflates the two. For those who favor Intelligent Design, religious faith trumps scientific reasoning and must be offered as a competing explanation for creation and evolution. Second, from a theological standpoint, Intelligent Design does not account for God's continuing creation. As I have suggested earlier, it is Haught's position that theology must engage with the best developments of science. This engagement results in what Haught names as developments in natural theology and the emergence of "evolutionary theology," and each has implications for a theology of God. Natural theology looks for evidence of God in nature, and this approach has been given new life in the emergence of the New Universe Story. The magnificence and complexity of the universe on both macro and micro levels gives the believer more reason for praise of the Creator of this universe. Evolutionary theology "seeks to show how our new awareness of cosmic and biological evolution can enhance and enrich traditional teaching about God and God's way of acting in the world."[45]

A doctrine of grace in this line of thought touches deeply on a theology of God—it is helpful to say a word about it. Grace, in this model, suggests that God loves the world (taken from the biblical witness), and allows the world to be exactly as it is—evolving gradually over vast amounts of time, with chance and natural selection as part of its dynamics. The relationship of love that God has with the

---

[44] See Haught, chap. 11, "Darwin and God after Dover," in *God after Darwin* for an extensive presentation on the Intelligent Design argument.

[45] Haught, *God after Darwin*, 40.

world suggests that God does not overwhelm the world with presence, but withdraws from the world paradoxically to be nearer to it. Haught argues that "God is present in the mode of 'hiddenness,' not abdication."[46] In process theology, which actively works to incorporate an evolutionary approach, God's power and grace is treated as "the capacity to influence"; it is power that expresses itself as persuasive love rather than force. With this understanding, we should not be surprised that creation unfolds in an experimental fashion over long periods of time. This suggests that God not only created the universe but continues to create it as it evolves.

Haught argues that, in a sense, we have distanced ourselves from a biblical understanding of God, using the image of Caesar more than the carpenter from Nazareth as a model for God. God's *kenosis* or pouring out, Haught notes, is at the heart of the Christian understanding of revelation and the Trinity. This biblical revelation of a vulnerable, defenseless, and humble deity as exemplified in the life and death of Jesus Christ suggests a God of self-donation, a God who pours self out to the very world God has created and redeems. This brings us once again to the question of God's "suffering" for and with the whole cosmos, not just humanity. "An evolutionary theology," Haught says, "expands this picture of God's suffering so as to have it embrace also the struggles of the entire universe and not just our own species' brief history here. . . . [T]his can mean only that the vast evolutionary odyssey, with all of its travail, enjoyment, and creativity, is also God's own travail, enjoyment, and creativity."[47]

An evolutionary theology of God also suggests that we depend less on a notion of a "prime mover" pushing things from the past, and more on God as "up ahead" or in the future, as Pierre Teilhard de Chardin encouraged. This will, Haught argues, give us evolution's own God. He suggests that we need a metaphysics of the future rather than of the past or even the present. "Evolution . . . seems to require a divine source of being that resides not in a timeless present located somewhere 'up above,' but in the future, essentially 'up ahead,' as the goal of a world still in the making."[48] This is a strong biblical

---

[46] Ibid., 43.
[47] Ibid., 55.
[48] Ibid., 91.

image of God best exemplified by the story of God leading Abraham and Sarah into an unknown future. In addition, we must pull from our scriptural sources the biblical hope for a new creation. Rather than being fixed on an ideal perfect past or even the present, a metaphysics of the future points to a "constantly arriving and renewing future."[49] It is the coming of the God of the future toward us that brings us hope. But this is not just for us, for as Paul states, the entire universe is groaning in expectation of that fullness to come.

Finally, Haught argues that we should never lose sight of our actual religious experience of God as self-emptying love and bearer of promise. Again, this is our biblical faith, and it is consonant with contemporary scientific understanding. This brings us back once again to God's relationship with the world. The God of love is an alluring force of the future, calling all creation to a certain autonomy so as not to overwhelm it with power. It is an approach that lets the beloved "be." "So if ultimate reality is essentially self-giving, and if love in turn entails 'letting the other be,' then . . . both the world's original coming into being and its indeterminate Darwinian transformation through time would be completely consonant with the Christian experience of God."[50] God creates the world as distinct from God's self, giving it the autonomy and freedom to develop according to the laws of chance, complexification, and self-organization. This voluntary distancing of God is precisely God's way of presence and involvement.

In summary, Haught argues for a God who is a wellspring of novelty; who is large enough to encompass the New Universe Story; who allows the world to be exactly as it is and does not overwhelm it with presence, but influences through persuasive love. This God is a kenotic God, pouring out self in a way that embraces the sufferings and joys of the whole universe and coming at the world "from ahead," calling it to a future of fulfillment.

[49] Ibid., 95.
[50] Ibid., 120.

Chapter 4

The Creator Spirit and the Big Bang

"I believe in the Holy Spirit, the Lord, the giver of life, / who proceeds from the Father and the Son, / who with the Father and the Son is adored and glorified, / who has spoken through the prophets." The Nicene Creed, the creed which Christian believers profess each week, encapsulates the faith of the church in the Holy Spirit. A theology of God's Spirit has roots in the Old Testament, where it is often referred to as the creative Spirit of God (e.g., Gen 1:2; 2:7; Ps 104:29-30); the Hebrew word *ruach*, often associated with the Spirit and meaning breath or wind, speaks of the life-giving power of God that hovered over the waters of chaos at the dawn of creation and gave life to the dry bones of Ezekiel (Ezek 47:1-13). The Spirit of God is also associated with the prophets, both in the capacity of judgment and promise. Micah declares, "But, as for me, I am filled with power, with the Spirit of the Lord, and with justice and might" (Mic 3:8); Isaiah proclaims "Here is my servant, whom I uphold, my chosen, in whom my soul delights; I have put my spirit upon him; he will bring forth justice to the nations" (Isa 42:1).

While a theology of the Spirit is incipient in the Old Testament, the New Testament witnesses to a much more developed theology of the Spirit, which in turn leads to a full trinitarian theology. The scenes of Jesus' baptism by John the Baptist attest to the Spirit's role in identifying Jesus and his relationship with God the Father (Matt 3:13-17; Mark 1:9-11; Luke 3:21-22; and John 1: 25-34). Jesus is the "beloved

Son" in whom "God is well pleased." Jesus is also one who will come baptizing with the Holy Spirit. The Spirit drives/leads Jesus into the desert and is with him as he begins his ministry: "The Spirit of the Lord is upon me, because he has anointed me to bring good news to the poor" (Luke 4:18). At his death Jesus hands over his Spirit (John 19:30), and gives the Spirit to the disciples with the commission to continue his saving work (John 20:21-23). The Acts of the Apostles is replete with mention of the Spirit, the force that empowers and guides the church from Jerusalem to the ends of the earth.

The trinitarian faith of the Christian community is well grounded in the scriptures and the liturgical life of the apostolic communities, but it receives much more explicit development in the early centuries of the church, when the distinctive identity and roles for the Father, Son, and Spirit are worked out, particularly at, between, and imme-diately after the Councils of Nicea (325) and Constantinople (381). The Cappadocians (Basil, Gregory of Nazianzus, and Gregory of Nyssa) as well as Athanasius and Didymus the Blind in the East, and Hilary, Ambrose, and Augustine in the West were primarily respon-sible for deepening the theology of the Spirit.

Basil contributed the idea that the Holy Spirit was to be adored and glorified. Gregory of Nazianzus concluded that if the former were true, the Spirit is truly God. Gregory of Nyssa provided the language that the Father, Son, and Spirit were one in being (*ousia*), and three in subsistence (*hypostasis*, Latin *persona*). These positions were ratified at the Council of Constantinople. Augustine, seeking a deeper understanding of the Holy Spirit, came to the conclusion in his work *On the Trinity* that the Spirit is primarily associated with love, the love of the Father and the Son. The Spirit is the unifying bond of love in the Trinity, and with humankind and the church. The addition to the Nicene-Constantinopolitan creed that the Spirit pro-ceeds from the Father *and the Son* (the *filioque* controversy) effectively split the West and the East and remains to this day a point of conten-tion between the churches. After the Patristic Period, the West ex-perienced a gradual impoverishment of the theology of the Spirit, particularly so after the Reformation.

The Second Vatican Council serves as a turning point in our atten-tion to the Spirit. Not only did the council extend the understanding of the Spirit's role in the life of the church, it also noted that the Spirit works outside the boundaries of the Christian Church. "For since

Christ died for everyone, and since all are in fact called to one and the same destiny, which is divine, we must hold that the holy Spirit offers to all the possibility of being made partners, in a way known to God, in the paschal mystery" (*Gaudium et Spes* 22). Numerous scholars have turned their attention to the Holy Spirit since the time of the council, and here we consider two who have attended to the relationship of the Spirit with the New Cosmology.

Denis Edwards on the Creator Spirit

Denis Edwards begins his study on the Creator Spirit by founding his work on the theology of Basil of Caesarea.[1] Edwards's argument is that Basil understands God as Communion and the Spirit as the Breath of God who always accompanies the Word, and when placed in dialogue with the New Science, will provide a renewed theology of the Spirit. The main ideas Edwards takes from Basil are that the Spirit is fully divine and that the Three are equally to be praised and glorified as our liturgical tradition gives witness.[2] *Koinonia* or communion defines the relationship of the three persons of the Trinity; they are distinct but complete mutuality marks their relationship. "For Basil, then, God is to be understood as radically relational."[3] The second idea Edwards takes from Basil is the image of the Spirit as the "breath of God who always accompanies the Word." Basil says:

> Christ comes, and the Spirit prepares his way. He comes in the flesh, but the Spirit is never separated from him. Working of miracles and gifts of healing come from the Holy Spirit. Demons are driven out by the Spirit of God. The presence of the Spirit despoils the devil. Remission of sins is given through the gift of the Spirit.[4]

In addition, Basil considers the Spirit as Sanctifier, as Life-Giver, and as Completer. Complementary to his emphasis on communion in the Trinity, Basil also emphasizes the communal nature of the Body

---

[1] Denis Edwards, *Breath of Life: A Theology of the Creator Spirit* (Maryknoll, NY: Orbis Books, 2004).

[2] Ibid., 23.

[3] Ibid., 25.

[4] Basil, *On the Holy Spirit* 19.49, as quoted in Edwards, *Breath of Life*, 27.

of Christ when he speaks about the gift of the Spirit to the church. As Edwards says, "It [communion] is also the mode of the Spirit's communication with creatures. . . . The Breath of God dwells *in* each creature, enabling each to share in the existence and life that come from the divine communion."[5]

With this as background, Edwards explores a theology of the Creator Spirit in terms of the New Science. It is his position that the story of the Spirit does not begin with Pentecost but with the origins of the Big Bang.[6] The Breath of God enabled the universe to exist and to evolve from the first second of creation. It is the Spirit of God who breathed life into the Big Bang, into the emergence of the first atoms, gases, and molecules; the first galaxies, stars, and nebulas; the formation of earth and its creatures; the first primates, our hominid ancestors, and modern humans. "The Spirit of God is creatively at work in the whole process celebrating every emergence, loving life in all its fecundity and diversity, treasuring it in its every instance."[7]

The Creator Spirit is also the sanctifier, gracing all of existence from all time. From the first humans, the Spirit offers grace in such a way that we can accept or reject this offer of love.[8] The Spirit is also in communion with the universe as it emerges in fecundity, beauty, and cooperation, but also in predation, competition, and death. In an emerging universe, death is the price paid for evolution. Christianity does not have an answer to suffering and death; it has only the witness of Jesus' death, which reveals a God who enters the pains of a limited universe and who promises life beyond death in resurrection hope. This includes the understanding that God self-limits out of love, taking into account the proper autonomy and independence of creation.[9] The Spirit accompanies creation as it emerges with all its travail, assisting and enabling the birth of the new. Using the female image from Romans 8:22, Edwards claims that the Spirit is like a midwife: "groaning with groaning creation as the new is being born."[10]

---

[5] Edwards, *Breath of Life*, 30.
[6] Ibid., 171.
[7] Ibid., 172.
[8] Ibid., 172–73.
[9] Ibid., 174.
[10] Ibid., 175.

The Spirit is also one who accompanies every creature and each creature's environment. The Spirit knows the experience of all things and grieves when destruction endangers the welfare of any element. Edwards suggests that because of the unique relationship of humanity with the Spirit (communion), humanity is also kin to other creatures.[11] All is related: every cell, organism, community, and system; all are held in the communion of the Spirit. The Spirit also "makes space" within the trinitarian relations for the emergence of the universe. As we have seen above, Edwards's is a pan*en*theistic approach which holds all in God without ever limiting God to creation. The divine Trinity is "the 'place' of the unfolding of the universe."[12] As contemporary science has grown in its appreciation of the interrelatedness of all things, so too has Christian theology stressed the mutual relations within the Trinity. When these two insights are brought together, Edwards suggests, "a view of reality emerges in which the entities that make up our universe can be understood as emergent and relational, as having their own integrity, and as evolving within the dynamic of divine life."[13]

In spite of the Spirit's closeness to all reality, the Spirit remains wild and uncontrollable. As mysterious as nature is, the God of creation is even more so. God always remains incomprehensible mystery. God is also infinitely personal. As Edwards argues, to say that the Spirit is personal is to say that the Spirit is radically relational.[14] He goes on to argue that not only is the Spirit a personal *presence*, it is also a *counterpart*. By this he means that the Spirit is a personal other with whom we can relate in love. But the Spirit's immanence extends beyond the human to all creation, and binds us all as kin. "To be in communion with this Spirit is to be in communion with all of God's creatures."[15]

In summary, Edwards argues that Basil's theology of the Spirit, when placed in dialogue with the New Science, will provide a renewed theology of the Spirit. God is understood as radically relational, and

[11] Ibid.
[12] Ibid., 176.
[13] Ibid.
[14] Ibid., 178.
[15] Ibid., 179.

the *koinonia* that characterizes life within the Trinity also marks the relationship of the Spirit with all creation. By virtue of that communion, we are in relation with all creation. The Spirit of God enabled the universe to exist from the beginning, and holds together all in existence in all its emergence and fecundity. The Creator Spirit graces all of existence, and graces the human community in such a way as to allow us the freedom to accept or reject that offer of love. God is one with creation in its joys as well as its travails; God self-limits out of love, allowing all creation its proper autonomy and freedom. Edwards holds a pan*en*theistic stance toward God's relation with creation; the Spirit makes space within the trinitarian relations of mutual love for the universe's emergence. The Spirit's immanence in all creation binds all together in a relationship of community; we are all kin to one another. Finally, Edwards argues that God is infinitely personal and acts as the other with whom we relate.

Elizabeth Johnson on the Creator Spirit

Feminist theologian Elizabeth Johnson addresses a theology of the Creator Spirit from an ecological perspective. After synthesizing material on the vast degradation of the earth and its systems of life, Johnson traces the possible causes of this ecocide. She credits hierarchical dualism as the taproot of the crisis, along with the patriarchal treatment of women that links women with nature/matter. The larger New Universe Story and the New Science are not Johnson's direct concern in her earlier work *Women, Earth, and Creator Spirit*, but she does reference them in her exploration of a theology of the Spirit. In her book *Quest for the Living God* she engages the New Cosmology more directly.[16] It is to the topic of the Creator Spirit and divine agency that I will now turn my attention.

In *Women, Earth, and Creator Spirit,* Johnson begins by asking the question "What must the Creator be like, in whose image this astounding universe is created?"[17] Her response is that we will be well served by turning to the person of the Spirit as we consider the rela-

---

[16] Elizabeth Johnson, *Women, Earth, and Creator Spirit* (Mahwah, NJ: Paulist Press, 1993); *Quest for the Living God* (New York: Continuum International, 2007).

[17] Johnson, *Women, Earth, and Creator Spirit*, 40.

tionship of God to the universe. The most primordial attribute that theology gives to the Spirit is that "the Spirit is the creative origin of all life."[18] From this flow three other insights: 1) the Creator Spirit is immanent in the historical world; 2) when things get broken, the Creative Spirit assumes the role of rejuvenating energy that renews the face of the earth; 3) because of the ongoing changes in historical life, the Spirit moves.[19] Following this, she explores the tradition for images of this Creator Spirit, and finds a rich collection of cosmic and female symbols.

The three most important cosmic symbols are wind, fire, and water. The Hebrew word for spirit is *ruach*. We find it described in images as small as a gentle breeze to as powerful as the winds that dried up the Red Sea. Importantly *ruach* is connected to the breath that gives life to all living things. "The whole community of creation," she says, "is sustained by the breath, the Spirit of God, who 'rides on the wings of the wind'" (Ps 104:3).[20] The Spirit is also symbolized by fire. It is at once mysterious, dangerous, and life sustaining. In the scriptures we have the burning bush that is not consumed; we have the tongues of fire on the heads of the disciples in the Upper Room, strengthening them to go out and proclaim the new life of the resurrection. Johnson connects the symbol of fire with the Big Bang, stating that the act of creation "is already a Pentecost, a first and permanent outpouring of the fiery Spirit of life."[21] Water too is a powerful, mysterious bringer of life and death. God, through the prophet Ezekiel, speaks of the people finding their true heart when God will sprinkle them with clean water and pour out a new spirit on them. For the Samaritan woman, Jesus promises a fountain of living water. In sum, as Johnson notes, "the Spirit is life that gives life. She is radiant life energy that like wind, fire, and water awakens and enlivens all things."[22]

Not only does the natural world give images for the Spirit's life and power; women's lives also offer rich symbolism for the Spirit's work. Johnson argues that "The female figure of Wisdom is the most

---

[18] Ibid., 42.
[19] Ibid., 43–44.
[20] Ibid., 47.
[21] Ibid., 48.
[22] Ibid., 50.

acutely developed personification of God's presence and activity in the Hebrew Scriptures." [23] In the book of Wisdom (7:22-23) she is described in twenty-one attributes from "intelligent, holy, unique" to "all-powerful, overseeing all, and penetrating through all other intelligent spirits." Wisdom is so associated with the creative work of God that she is described as the "fashioner of all things" (Wis 7:22). "She reaches mightily from one end of the earth to the other, and she orders all things well" (Wis 8:1). She "renews all things" and binds all things together in communion: "in every generation she passes into holy souls and makes them friends of God, and prophets" (Wis 7:27). In spite of the fact that this Wisdom tradition has been in the shadows in the Christian tradition, Johnson notes that "virtually every aspect of the Creator Spirit's activity in the world, as delineated in doctrine and theology, is depicted in the wisdom literature in female symbolism." [24]

Female bodily imagery is also a vehicle for expressing the Spirit's relationship with the world. The Spirit is the "great, creative Matrix" that grounds and sustains the cosmos and entices it toward its future. Responding to the universe that is at once self-organizing and self-transcending, the Spirit empowers the cosmos from within. "The Spirit's action does not supplant that of creatures but works cooperatively in and through created actions, random, ordered, or free." [25] Like many of the theologians referenced above, Johnson speaks of the Spirit's compassion with the universe's travails, but she does so in feminine imagery. "When creation groans in labor pains and we do too (Rom 8:22-23), the Spirit is in the groaning and in the midwifing that breathes rhythmically along and cooperates in the birth." [26] Finally, Johnson argues that a theology of Creator Spirit overcomes the dualism of matter and spirit, thereby contributing to a sense of the sacredness of the earth. Instead of matter being divorced from spirit and denigrated, it is, Johnson argues, an intrinsic and honored part of the cosmic community.

[23] Ibid., 52.
[24] Ibid., 54.
[25] Ibid., 58.
[26] Ibid., 59.

In her *Quest for the Living God*, Johnson takes on the question of divine agency. Taking her lead from the fact that the cosmos is at once enormously old, large, complex, and dynamic, Johnson joins the debate on the agency of God in such a cosmos.[27] Summing up five different positions, she points to the fact that all these positions share the conviction that the Creator Spirit empowers the process of evolution from within. "They see divine creativity active," she says, "*in, with, and under* cosmic processes. God makes the world . . . by empowering the world to make itself."[28] This is in the face of the challenge that science poses by suggesting that the cosmos works by law and by chance. In other words, in addition to the laws of nature, there is an openness to the cosmic processes that makes them intrinsically unpredictable. This is witnessed to in quantum physics by its "uncertainty principle." Chaos theory offers another place for such randomness in the butterfly effect. And natural selection has its own form of randomness with genetic mutation and changes in environment that lead development in new directions. Given these parameters and deep time, the cosmos can offer up the radically new, and "more" can come from "less." Where does God's agency come in here?

Johnson argues that "as boundless love at work in the ongoing evolution of the universe, divine creativity is the source not just of cosmic order but also of the chance that allows novelty to appear."[29] The indwelling Spirit of God exercises agency not only through the laws of the universe but through chance occurrence and randomness as well. As Johnson says, "In the emergent evolutionary universe, we should not be surprised to find divine creativity hovering very close to turbulence."[30] She, like several of the authors we have considered above, takes the Christ model of divine *kenosis* to explain how God allows creation to transcend itself even with the limitation of suffering and death. God's suffering in, with, and through creation is not a sign of impotence but a sign of self-offering love poured out in solidarity with all creation.

[27] Johnson, *Quest for the Living God*, 192–93. See especially her discussion on the multiple positions on this question.

[28] Ibid., 193, italics in original.

[29] Ibid., 195.

[30] Ibid., 195.

In summary, Johnson reviews the evidence in scripture that gives a picture of the Creator Spirit in relationship with God and with the cosmos. The Spirit is the source of all life, is immanent in the world, renews the face of the earth, and is a moving force throughout the cosmos. The Spirit is effectively imaged as wind, fire, and water, bringing life mysteriously to those open to the Spirit's promptings. The female figure of Wisdom is a rich source of knowing the Spirit's action. She is present from the creation of the world and orders all things well. Using female imagery again, the Spirit is depicted as groaning and midwifing the birth of new creation. The Creator Spirit overcomes the dualism of matter and spirit and overcomes the negative ramifications of that dualism in the world.

Johnson also addresses the question of divine agency in the face of the universe's age, size, complexity, and dynamism. She argues that the Creator Spirit works within the processes of both law and chance, enabling the universe's existence, continuous development, and ultimate future.

Chapter 5

Christology and the Big Bang

Like the theology of the Holy Spirit, a classical theology of Christ or Christology was forged in the centuries immediately following the apostolic period and the witness of the New Testament.[1] Christological developments reached a climax by the end of the fifth century and can be traced by following the controversies regarding Jesus' humanity, his divinity, his nature, and his salvific efficacy.

The first major controversy was that of Arius's denial of the divinity of the Logos in the early fourth century. Arius, a priest of Alexandria, argued that the Logos was created out of nothing as the highest creature but, as created, was not divine. The Logos was not of the same substance as the Father. Even though Arius was condemned in 320, his position found wide support, which in turn called for further action. The first ecumenical council was called in 325 at Nicea to deal with the issue of Arianism. The Council declared that the Son is "true God from true God, begotten not made, of one substance (*homoousios*) with the Father," thus settling the question of the Son's divinity. The controversies of the end of the fourth century and fifth century centered more on the integrity of Christ's humanity and the reality of the crucifixion. Apollinarius, bishop of Laodicea from ca. 360, argued

---

[1] See John P. Galvin, "Jesus Christ," in *Systematic Theology: Roman Catholic Perspectives*, vol. 1, ed. Francis Schüssler Fiorenza and John P. Galvin (Minneapolis, MN: Fortress Press, 1991), 251–324, for an in-depth look at the development of classical Christology.

that Christ's humanity lacked its own active principle; the soul of Christ was replaced by the Logos. The First Council of Constantinople (381) condemned this position and settled the question of Jesus' full humanity. As the fifth century approached, issues arose about the unity of the two natures of Christ and Mary as the *Theotokos*. The Council of Chalcedon in 451 resolved many of these issues by professing both the unity of Christ and the completeness of his divinity and humanity, and affirming that Mary could be called *Theotokos* in reference to Christ's humanity. Chalcedon provided important language in the development of orthodox Christology: "One and the same Christ, Son, Lord, Only begotten, made known in two natures (which exist) without confusion, without change, without division, without separation." This understanding of Christ as one "in two natures" or that the two natures are united in one person (*prosopon*) and one hypostasis effectively rejected the position of monophysitism. With the Third Council of Constantinople (680–81), classical Christological doctrine was set. There were no significant developments in Christological doctrine in the medieval period.

There was a contemporary resurgence in Christology beginning in 1951 when the church celebrated the fifteen hundredth anniversary of Chalcedon.[2] Two things affected the reconsideration of Christ: first, the turn to the subject, and second, reflection on the horrors of the twentieth century—the Holocaust, the threat of nuclear war, ecological disaster, etc. As Elizabeth Johnson suggests, this resulted in a "recovery of the relevance of Jesus' ministry with his preaching of the reign of God, a symbol with social and political implications."[3] The Christian community began to ask how "praxis . . . become[s] a path of knowledge about Jesus Christ."[4] New questions also arose regarding the relevance of Christ to those practicing other religions and to the millions following no religion at all. Concern for the vast amount of human suffering and natural and human-made disasters raised questions about Jesus' solidarity with the whole earth community, indeed the whole universe. Liberation Christology moved

---

[2] See Elizabeth Johnson, *Consider Jesus: Waves of Renewal in Christology* (New York: Crossroad, 1990), for a concise summary of the contemporary developments in Christology.

[3] Ibid., 13.

[4] Ibid.

reflection from white males to those on the "underside" of history. Latin American Liberation theology, as well as that from Africa and Asia, along with feminist and womanist theological reflection raised questions regarding justice and the Christ, and how discipleship must result in changed praxis. Developments in ecology were also placed in dialogue with Christology, also with an emphasis on changed praxis. This attention to Jesus Christ and the fate of the earth leads us to consider Christology in light of the New Science and the New Cosmic Story.

Ilia Delio on Christology

Ilia Delio shapes her Christology in terms of moving from the first Axial Period to the second Axial Period of which I spoke earlier.[5] She too is convinced that Christianity must take into account that in this second Axial Period we are moving into a world that is globally conscious, ecologically sensitive, communal, and mindful of the evolution of the whole cosmos. Christology, which was formed within Greek thought patterns and continued to develop within a medieval cosmology, must be rethought from the perspective of an evolutionary cosmos if it is to be taken seriously in this second Axial Period. Delio argues that Christology, and indeed all theology, is local in that it is always formed within a particular historical, social, philosophical, and political context.[6] Her concern is that since our situation has changed so significantly because of the New Science, we perhaps no longer have an operative Christology that speaks to our world. Her task is to develop a contextual Christology, a cosmic Christology, for our age. Some of her dialogue partners for this task are Bonaventure, Teilhard de Chardin, and Karl Rahner.

From the Franciscan Bonaventure, she draws on his grounding of a theology of creation and of Christ in the nature of God as Trinity. Regarding creation, she summarizes Bonaventure as saying that "God could not communicate being to the finite if he were not supremely communicative in himself."[7] For Bonaventure there is an integral

---

[5] This summary is taken from *Christ in Evolution* (Maryknoll, NY: Orbis Books, 2008) and *The Emergent Christ* (Maryknoll, NY: Orbis Books, 2011).

[6] Delio, *Christ in Evolution*, 29.

[7] Ibid., 58.

relation between the Trinity and creation in that "God's nature as primal, fecund mystery of self-communication makes possible all of God's work *ad extra*."[8] All of creation, from the smallest to the largest elements, reflects the Trinity as its origin, reason for existence, and end. This leads to a sacramental view of all creation; each and every creature is a potential sacrament of God's presence and trinitarian life.

Regarding Christ and creation, Bonaventure discerns a relationship between the mode of the incarnation of the divine Son and the mystery of creation. Delio argues that in the incarnation, "God completes what God initiates in creation and crowns it with eternal significance."[9] For Bonaventure, Christ and the world are not accidentally but intrinsically related. "Just as the divine Word is the inner self-expression of God, the created order is the external expression of the inner Word."[10] There is no necessity for the incarnation, only God's trinitarian love that is expressed *ad extra* in the world. In other words, humankind's sin is not the reason for the sending of the Word; God intended to express the Word in Jesus totally out of love for creation. In this sense, "the humanity of Jesus is the fullest embodiment of that self-utterance within the created world. . . . The humanity of Jesus is the fullest and most perfect external Word that gives expression to the inner, eternal Word as its perfect content."[11]

The implications of this Christology for our own world are that it suggests our evolutionary world is meaningful and purposeful because it is grounded in Christ. In addition, all reality is united in Christ; it is a true cosmos centered in Christ, not a mere collection of individual entities. Quoting Bonaventure interpreter Zachary Hayes, Delio highlights the relationship between what happens between the world and Christ and what happens to created reality. "The intrinsic relationship between Christ and creation means that 'what happened between God and the world in Christ points to the future of the cosmos. It is a future that involves the radical transformation of created reality through the unitive power of God's love.'"[12] The universe will

---

[8] Ibid., 58.

[9] Ibid., 60.

[10] Ibid.

[11] Ibid., 59.

[12] Zachary Hayes, "Christ, Word of God and Exemplar of Humanity," *Cord* 46, no. 1 (1996): 12. As quoted in Delio, *Christ in Evolution*, 64.

not be destroyed, but will have a destiny that was intended from the beginning and was anticipated in the incarnate Word and glorified Christ. What happened to Jesus in the resurrection is the model for what will happen to the universe.

Delio draws out from Teilhard de Chardin that "Christ is not only at the heart of the universe, but at the heart of the material universe."[13] All matter contains an internal dynamism toward spirit. In addition, evolution follows a movement from autonomy to organization or relatedness. Creation, according to Teilhard, is also oriented toward maximal human organization and consciousness—the risen Christ. In other words, while humanity is the growing tip of an evolutionary movement, Christ is the exemplar of the ultimate goal of emergence. As Delio summarizes, "By taking on human form, Christ has given the world its definitive form: he has been consecrated for a cosmic function. The convergence of evolution toward greater complexity organized around a personal center meant for Teilhard that the very physical process of evolution has within it a centrating principle, which is Christ."[14] It is Christ the Evolver "*who is in evolution* is himself the *cause and center* of evolution and its goal."[15] In her most recent work, Delio picks up Teilhard's more radical idea that God is in process and the universe contributes something to the fullness of God. "Evolution is not only the universe coming to be but it is *God* who is *coming to be.*"[16] This is in the context of saying that the traditional metaphysics of being is inadequate to an evolutionary world that experiences pain, suffering, and death. In speaking about the suffering and death of Jesus, Delio quotes theologian William Thompson, who suggests that "Jesus radicalized the Hebraic entry into axial consciousness. . . . [His] death glaringly sums up what such a consciousness entails"; it is the intensification of what is involved in this-worldly responsibility.[17] Delio also shows how a cosmic Christology is affected by taking evolution into account. Not only do we claim that Jesus is the immediacy of God's presence, but that "in his death

[13] Delio, *Christ in Evolution*, 68–69.
[14] Ibid., 71.
[15] Delio, *The Emergent Christ*, 50, italics in original.
[16] Ibid., 52, italics in original.
[17] As quoted in *The Emergent Christ*, 56.

and resurrection, the power of God [is present] to conquer all forces threatening to destroy not only human individuation but human relatedness. In Jesus there emerged a new sense of what it means to belong to the cosmos."[18] Delio goes on to talk about the primacy of Christ in evolution. Christ does not intervene in evolution, she suggests; rather

> the whole evolutionary process is incarnational. Evolution is *christogenesis* or God coming to be at the heart of matter, but it is also *theogenesis* because it is *God* coming to be at the heart of matter.[19]

Karl Rahner is also an important conversation partner for Delio. Basing her thought on Rahner's theology of symbol, Delio explores Jesus as symbol. He is, she suggests, symbol of the potential of every human person for unity with God. Christ is the symbol of God in that he is the "Word of God expressed or projected outward in space, time, and history. . . . The symbol of Christ functions as the meaning of God for us and discloses to us the true meaning of our lives in God. Christ is the symbol of the Trinitarian mystery of God. . . ."[20] Christ also symbolizes the capacity of all of us to be united and transformed in God.[21] Christ is the New Being because he mediates the "power of an undisrupted union that heals divisions and separations and creates reunion of one's self with one's self and with the family of creation."[22]

Extending her own thought beyond that of her conversation partners, Delio suggests that as simple isolated structures must die for the sake of more complex unions, "so too, Christology as a Western (and hence isolated) doctrine is undergoing a transformation, a complexification, through the evolution of human (and Christian) consciousness."[23] The global consciousness that characterizes the second Axial Period demands a new Christology, and in her mind, spiritu-

---

[18] Delio, *The Emergent Christ*, 56.
[19] Ibid., 53, italics in original.
[20] Delio, *Christ in Evolution*, 127.
[21] Delio, *The Emergent Christ*, 88.
[22] Ibid., 92.
[23] Delio, *Christ in Evolution*, 123.

ality must be at the heart of this new cosmic Christology. Spirituality, she argues, "or the 'doing of Christ' in the world today, must be the source of understanding Christ in this new age."[24] Only those willing to enter into the mystery of Christ can come to "know" who Christ is. Basing theological reflection on experience is not a new concept (she calls it vernacular theology), but it is new in our contemporary context of evolution, religious plurality, and difference. While traditional Christology arising out of the first Axial Period dealt with the humanity and divinity of Christ, the Christology of the second Axial Period must address the cosmic nature of Christ. Can we understand the person of Jesus, she asks, "as the evolutionary divine emergent in history, not only as the mysterious union of natures, but as the integrated being in whom a new field of activity arises that promotes wholeness and evolution toward God? Can we see Jesus as the exemplar of relatedness for the fullness of evolutionary life?"[25]

Indeed, Delio does see such a Christology as possible. What happened in Jesus was a new kind of consciousness and relatedness to God which ushers in "a new way of being God-centered, earth-centered, and in communion with one another."[26] This requires conversion and commitment, as his disciples learned, that are at once dangerous to the principalities and powers, and yet instill a freedom precisely in the face of such danger.

Delio also suggests that a new way of understanding Jesus is that of *whole-maker*. For Jesus to make whole was to heal physical, emotional, and spiritual divisions, not only with individuals but with communities. Health, then, is to be in right relationship, exhibiting compassion, peace, and forgiveness. A healthy cosmos, Delio writes, "[r]equires healthy people who live in openness, compassionate love, and receptivity to others, accepting others as part of self because we are one in the depth of God's love."[27] Jesus' commitment to this kind of love led him, and leads us, to the cross, which Delio suggests is also God's passion. The cross of Christ "reveals the total self-giving love of God that reaches out to estranged humanity and embraces

---

[24] Ibid., 125.
[25] Delio, *The Emergent Christ*, 46.
[26] Ibid., 62.
[27] Ibid., 65.

every stranger as the beloved."[28] For Delio, this is the meaning of eucharist. It is a sacrament of evolution "because every act of Eucharist is an act of making a new future through a new divine presence, a new relatedness, a new freedom to love. . . . Whole-making is the desire to be part of a greater whole, and Eucharist sacramentalizes the whole."[29]

Delio also argues that Christ can no longer be seen as contained by one particular group or even related only to humanity. The meaning of Christ, she argues, "is the divinization of the whole cosmos." In addition, "Christ's reality is not exhausted with Jesus' historicity. Jesus is the Christ, but Christ is more than Jesus because 'Christ is that central symbol that incorporates the whole of reality.'"[30] While some are moving to post-Christianity, Delio argues with Raimon Panikkar that our current Christology must be inclusive and not be limited to a misreading of Jesus as a white, Western, male Jesus, for he was really Middle Eastern and Jewish. "Christ," she says, "is not merely *a* person but *the* person, the cosmic personal center of a God-directed universe. There can be no 'beyond Christ' because Christ alone is the fullness of what we hope for in God."[31]

Summing up, Delio locates Christ at the heart of the whole evolutionary process. Christ is more than the man Jesus: "he is the exemplar of creation, the centrating principle of evolution, and the Omega point of an evolutionary universe."[32] Every person and the whole of creation find meaning in Christ. Everything and everyone is related to Christ whether they know Christ or not. Christ is the symbol of all that humanity yearns for, all that the universe is evolving toward. Christ is the ground of all existence as well as the Omega point of its destiny. The Christ event, for Delio, is "an organic event; it is living, dynamic, and related to the physical and spiritual life unfolding in the universe."[33] In an evolutionary Christology, Christ's death and resurrection point toward the reality that God's presence conquers all forces that threaten to destroy human individuation and relatedness. In a cosmic Christology, Christ is the whole-maker, healing and

[28] Ibid., 67.
[29] Ibid., 68.
[30] Delio, *Christ in Evolution*, 128.
[31] Ibid., 135, italics in original.
[32] Ibid., 174.
[33] Ibid., 175.

reconciling individuals and communities; such action leads to the cross for him and his followers. Such costly love reveals a God who offers self to all of creation. Cosmic Christology has preconditions for Delio as well as consequences. First, anyone who wishes to theologize on the Christ must be steeped in spirituality and then move on to reflective theology, or as Rahner said, the Christian of the future must be a mystic. Second, Christians cannot limit their participation in Christ to the sacraments; they must participate in Christ in the world which is his expression.

Elizabeth Johnson on Christology

Elizabeth Johnson situates her treatment of Christology in an evolutionary context by addressing a vexing problem: how to understand the tremendous pain, suffering, and death that is part of an evolutionary cosmos distinct from any human responsibility (while not giving a theodicy or rationalizing). She is concerned not to conflate the ethical (human responsibility) with the biological fact of untold pain, waste, and death that is part and parcel of the emergence of new life. As she says, "Like pain and suffering, death is indigenous to the evolutionary process. . . . The time-limit that ticks away in all living organisms and ends with their death is deeply structured into the creative advance of life."[34] It is her conviction that theology must address itself to the biological reality of suffering and death, which, in her mind, it has not done sufficiently to date. Any theology that attempts to dialogue with Darwin and his scientific heirs must take this biological fact into account; consequently, it must address this question in any considerations of God or of Christology in particular.

As a point of departure, Johnson suggests that the most fundamental move theology can make "is to affirm the compassionate presence of God in the midst of the shocking enormity of pain and death."[35] For believers, the Giver of life must abide somehow in the pain, suffering, and death of creation. The good God must stand in solidarity with created reality precisely in its suffering and agony, and promise

---

[34] Elizabeth Johnson, *Ask the Beasts: Darwin and the God of Love* (London: Bloomsbury, 2014), 184.

[35] Ibid., 191.

something more. Death ought not to have the last word. The question arises of how that happens. For the Christian believer and theologian, one must turn for insight into the life, death, and resurrection of Jesus Christ. It is there that believers find the truest revelation of the living God. "In Christ," she explains, "the living God who creates and empowers the evolutionary world also enters the fray, personally drinking the cup of suffering and going down into the nothingness of death, to transform it from within."[36]

Johnson begins her theological reflection on the Christ by noting the connections the early church made with Jesus and Wisdom. It is in the person of Wisdom, who was there at the beginning of creation and who indwells all creatures, who feeds at her table and prevails over evil, that we gain insight into the relationship between God and creation. As Johnson argues, "personified Wisdom is one way of figuring the creative, revealing, and saving presence of God in engagement with the world."[37] But Wisdom was not the only image used. When the church first began discoursing about the Christ, it used the vocabulary of both Wisdom and Word to speak about the revelation of God in Christ. It is in the prologue to John's gospel (John 1:1-18) that we hear of Jesus' coming as the self-expressing Word of God in loving relationship with the world.

Johnson stresses that the vocabulary about Jesus' coming into the world in John's prologue is quite explicit. The Word did not become human (Gr. *anthropos*), or a man (Gr. *Aner*), but flesh (Gr. *sarx*). Unlike the propensity of Greek thought to honor spirit above flesh or matter, the early Christian community firmly proclaimed that the Word became part of material reality. Johnson argues that this was done with purpose: "the Word *became* flesh, entered into the sphere of the material to shed light on all from within."[38] This is the hermeneutical key to the Christology that she then develops. In addition, Johnson suggests that before we can develop a Christology in an evolutionary context, we must begin with an anthropology in that context. "We evolved relationally; we exist symbiotically; our existence depends on interaction with the rest of the natural world. . . . The flesh that

---

[36] Ibid., 192.
[37] Ibid., 193.
[38] Ibid., 195.

the Word of God became as a human being is part of the vast body of the cosmos."[39] Like others whom we have reviewed previously, the story of humankind can be told only within the larger story of the evolution of the whole cosmos. It is this story that the Word and Wisdom of God take on as his story.

Johnson uses the term "deep incarnation," a term coined by Niels Gregersen, to speak about the deep involvement of the *Logos* in the human condition with all its connotations of evolution, interdependence, suffering, and death. She argues that this involvement is done with purpose: "Now incarnation enacts a radical embodiment whereby the divine *Logos* joins the material world . . . in order to accomplish a new level of union between Creator and creature."[40] In other words, there is nothing in existence that the *Logos* has not assumed by taking on flesh (*sarx*). All the connections among the elements of the universe that science has recently uncovered are what Jesus Christ has taken on. " 'Deep incarnation' understands John 1:14 [and the Word became flesh] to be saying that the *sarx* which the Word of God became not only counts Jesus among other human beings; it also reaches beyond them to join him to the whole biological world of living creatures and the cosmic dust of which they are composed. The incarnation is a cosmic event."[41] This clearly is an example of the science/religion *conversation* bearing fruit in a renewed Christology.

By taking on flesh, God has taken on the history of the universe as part of God's own story. This also means that God has come to share in the limited experiences of all created life including suffering and death, knowing it from the inside. As Johnson writes, "This deep incarnation of God within the biotic community of life forges a new kind of union, one with different emphasis from the empowering communion created by the indwelling Creator Spirit. This is a union in the flesh."[42]

This leads us to a second step in a developing Christology. Through a wide variety of parables and natural images, Jesus invites people

[39] Ibid., 196.
[40] Ibid.
[41] Ibid., 197.
[42] Ibid., 198–99.

(particularly on the margins) to share in the good news of the reign of God. Johnson asks if reading the gospels with an ecological sensitivity might suggest that the good news "might include the land and its other creatures."[43] Her conclusion is that it *would* include the natural world. By taking on a body, Jesus gives value to all bodies, to all materiality. Without attributing an ecological sensitivity to Jesus living in the first century, his compassion understood in an evolutionary context extends beyond human elites to all of creation.

Johnson's third move is to consider the cross and the suffering of the Word made flesh. Through his suffering and death on the cross, the Word of God takes that suffering and death up into God. This is pushing classical Christology further than it usually goes. To those who would argue that there is no "suffering" in God, Johnson argues, "In his own body, he knows. Since he is Wisdom incarnate, this knowing is embedded in the very heart of the living God."[44] While she acknowledges that God is fullness of life beyond suffering, it is also right to say that "God suffered and died on the cross because the human nature of Jesus who suffered is that of the Word of God."[45] While this understanding of Jesus'/God's suffering links Christ in solidarity to all others who suffer and die, Johnson again asks the question of whether this solidarity extends to the whole community of life. She argues that it is warranted to extend this line of reasoning on God's solidarity with the suffering "into the groan of suffering and the silence of death of all creatures."[46] Such solidarity reveals God's perennial relation to creation. While solidarity does not take away suffering, Johnson argues with Christopher Southgate that such solidarity takes away "the aloneness of the suffering creature's experience."[47] The companioning of God's Spirit with all creation does not stop at its moment of suffering and death. "The cross," Johnson says, "gives warrant for locating the compassion of God right at the center of the affliction."[48]

[43] Ibid., 200.
[44] Ibid., 203.
[45] Ibid.
[46] Ibid., 205.
[47] Ibid., 206.
[48] Ibid.

Finally, Johnson addresses the question of whether death is the last word for humankind and for all of creation. Her logic goes once more to the experience of Jesus Christ to give us insight into the working of the relationship of God with humanity and the world. Jesus' resurrection gives witness to the creative power of love to transcend all limits, even that of death. The transformation he went through, his destiny, is proclaimed in the Christian scriptures as the destiny of all of us. He is "the firstborn from the dead" (Col 1:18). As Johnson notes, "In view of the solidarity of the human race, his destiny means that our hope does not merely clutch at a possibility but stands on an irrevocable ground of what has already transpired in him."[49] Classical eschatology suggests that all of us will be raised from the dead, our spirits and our matter, but what of the rest of creation? Does "deep incarnation" give way to "deep resurrection"? As one would suspect from her previous argumentation, Johnson replies to our question in the affirmative. "The evolving world of life, all of matter in its endless permutations, will not be left behind but will likewise be transfigured by the resurrecting action of the Creator Spirit."[50] Just as all life is from God, all transformation into that beyond-which-we-cannot-imagine is also from the Creator God.

In summary, Johnson situates her Christology in the larger evolutionary context by asking what we are to make of the tremendous pain, suffering, and death of all of creation as a biological necessity. She attempts to answer that question by exploring what we can learn about God's relationship with the world through the experience of Jesus Christ dead and risen. She argues that because the Word of God took on flesh, he took on the interrelated reality of all creation. The Word did not just become a human being, but a human being who is intrinsically matter and is related to everything else in the cosmos. His "deep incarnation" relates Jesus to the whole cosmos, and so his significance also relates to the whole cosmos. His solidarity is not just with the human community and its sufferings and joys but with the suffering and joys of all creation. Jesus' experience of suffering and death enables that experience to be taken "into God" in such a way that it is possible to honor God's impassability and that God "suffers."

[49] Ibid., 208.
[50] Ibid., 209.

God's solidarity with all creation means that death is not taken away, but that God is present to whatever suffering and limits apply in an evolutionary cosmos. Deep incarnation is met with deep resurrection in that the promise of transformation beyond death is made not only to the human community but to the whole of creation.

Part III

Implications for
Liturgical Theology and Praxis

While we could go on at greater length about how developments in theology have taken into account an evolutionary and ecological worldview, it is time to turn our attention to how liturgical theologians and practitioners can enter this ever-widening dialogue. I am suggesting that at this juncture, the systematic theologians of our churches are at the frontlines of integrating an evolutionary and ecological worldview into our belief systems and are outpacing anything in liturgical studies. This book is an attempt to engage liturgical studies in what Thomas Berry calls the "great work" of carrying out the transition from "a period of human devastation of the Earth" to a time when the human community will "be present to the planet in a mutually beneficial manner."[1] This ecological consciousness will be supplemented by an effort to engage the New Science and the New Cosmology.

In my review of developments in a theology of creation, God, the Holy Spirit, and Christology, two things are clear. On the one hand, an evolutionary and ecological worldview is not in competition with a biblical worldview. For those of us who are not biblical literalists, the myths of origins (or cosmogony) were never intended to be scientifically "correct," but were meant to ponder deep human questions of

---

[1] Thomas Berry, *The Great Work: Our Way into the Future* (New York: Bell Tower, 1999), 2.

81

purpose and meaning, origin, and destiny. In other words, conflict or even contrast between science and religion does not have to be the order of the day. However, this being said, it is also clear that in many instances our worship traditions express a cosmology or an understanding of the universe and our place in it that is outdated and insensitive to an ecological consciousness. While we do not have to accept unequivocally the accusation that the biblical mandate to "subdue the earth" has led to ecological disaster,[2] we must admit that our biblical and worship traditions have not been dominant forces in shaping an ecological consciousness in our culture. At least we must take responsibility for a lack of insight and leadership in this area to date.

In spite of the liturgical reforms of the Second Vatican Council, our newly shaped rites and revised texts do not reflect the *influence* of the New Cosmology. When most of the rites were being revised (late 1960s and 1970s), the *conversation* with the New Science had not yet matured. At the present moment, when we are experiencing a second round of liturgical revisions, new texts are not being admitted into the corpus of the liturgical books. Emphasis has been placed on a more direct translation of the *editio typica* (original Latin texts) texts. This is unfortunate since at the present time, it would have been opportune to work through the paradigm shift to a new cosmology within the worship practices of our faith tradition. One can only hope that in the foreseeable future, we will take the opportunity to do that integration. The challenge, as I see it, is complex and multifaceted, and needs to involve the whole spectrum of liturgical scholarship. We need those doing historical studies to critique our traditions and to raise up those elements that are compatible with an evolutionary and ecological worldview; and we need those who are responsible for shaping worship to develop prayers and rites that more prophetically call our communities to conversion and orthopraxis.

[2] See the seminal article by Lynn White, "The Historical Roots of Our Ecologic Crisis," *Science* 155 (1967): 1203–7. White argues that the Genesis text has led to ecological disaster.

Those engaged in the historical study of worship in the biblical traditions could explore the cosmological and ecological understandings of their respective prayer traditions. The first order of business would be to provide a critical reading of the tradition to see exactly what is expressed of a cosmology and to uncover the understanding of the relationship of humanity to nature. Since domination of humans over the earth has been traced to a parallel domination of men over women and an eliding of women with nature, such an effort would provide insight into where the tradition needs to be changed in order for it to foster the well-being of all of humanity and the cosmos. Such studies would be an invaluable service to those among us who are also responsible for shaping service books and worship traditions. While this historical work is an important agenda for the field of liturgical studies and praxis, it is beyond the limits of this text to do such an analysis. I invite my colleagues in historical studies to attend to this agenda.

Those who are in a position of making decisions regarding the content of worship services bear the responsibility of understanding the implications of an evolutionary and ecological worldview and what shape our prayer traditions might take in the future with these in mind. This work can be understood as providing pastoral care that has the potential for transforming minds and attitudes, and providing leadership in the development of right practice or orthopraxis. While the historical work logically seems to precede the more creative work, there is actually more movement within the creative dimension than with the historical at this time. It is to this more creative task that I will turn my attention in the coming pages. First, I will direct my comments to sacramentality and the sacraments of the Roman Catholic tradition. Then I will look at other places where creative efforts are going on regarding the New Cosmology, an ecological theology and liturgical praxis.

Chapter 6

Sacramentality and the New Cosmology

In chapter 1, I indicated that in the *lex orandi/lex credendi* debate, I was interested in the *influence* of the science and religion conversation on liturgical theology and liturgical practice. I turn now to the topic of sacramental theology, highlighting four aspects of it which reveal the influence of the New Cosmology on sacramentality in general terms. I will then explore several individual sacraments, and show how they are affected by the theological incorporation of the New Cosmology.

To begin, a sacramental theology suggests that God can be and is revealed, embodied, and communicated through created reality. A too exaggerated sacramentalism absolutizes nature and loses the distinction between Creator and creation (pantheism). However, a more balanced sacramentalism does not slip into pantheism, but finds God revealed, embodied, and communicated in created reality, even while God always exceeds those created limits. Many of the authors I have reviewed are convinced that this pan*en*theistic account of the relationship between God and the universe is a more appropriate approach. All exists in God, but God is never identified with creation. God always exceeds the created universe even while granting it apposite autonomy and even freedom.

While one could argue that there is nothing especially new in this description of sacramentality, the actual expansion of our knowledge of the universe causes us to reconsider our traditional understanding.

Sacramentality in light of the New Science must be a cosmic sacramentality that expands whatever we have developed to date to include the far reaches of the visible universe. We must include the immensely large, the infinitesimally small, the tremendously old, and the extremely complex as those elements which reveal God and embody God's care. For believers, nothing exceeds or limits God's desire for revelation and communication.

Second, sacramentality at its best demands that we take seriously our own materiality and the materiality of our ritual objects. Recently we have moved to a more integrated understanding of human persons. We are taking more seriously the intrinsic relationship between body and mind-soul-spirit, and not overvaluing one above the other. We are embodied spirits who can only be in the world through our bodies. We are sentient creatures who experience the world through the many senses that are part of embodied existence. In this regard, we are one with all other living forms, acting and interacting with our environment both natural and created. In addition, our bodies are made up of inorganic substances—minerals, water, oils, etc., which make us one with all created, inorganic life on this planet and in the universe. As we have said earlier, everything that exists had its origins in stardust. Regarding sacramentality, God reveals and communicates God's self to us in our embodied existence and through all matter of things that make up our environment. Human experience of God is mediated experience, mediated through our own embodiment and through creation.

Water, oil, fire, bread, wine, hands outstretched in blessing—the stuff of our sacramental life—all of these have a history, but a history beyond their use in the Hebrew and Christian Scriptures and in Jewish and Christian liturgical practice. Because of the developments in the New Science, our religious landscape is beginning to be contextualized in the cosmic. As Linda Gibler so wonderfully demonstrates in her text *From the Beginning to Baptism: Scientific and Sacred Stories of Water, Oil, and Fire,*[1] the history of these objects can be traced from the Big Bang through the creation of basic elements, stars, galaxies, and planets, to the emergence of life on this planet and the development of consciousness in the first humans, and then to our own reli-

---

[1] Linda Gibler, *From the Beginning to Baptism: Scientific and Sacred Stories of Water, Oil, and Fire* (Collegeville, MN: Liturgical Press, 2010).

gious traditions. God's revelation comes to us through the molecules of water, the oil of cell membranes, and the fire that lights the universe, our solar system, our Earth, and our own bodies. As Gibler indicates, "a cosmocentric sacramentality is one that fully believes that God is truly present to and in each aspect of creation, that the Universe is God-drenched."[2] The cosmos is now the context within which we can understand the church's seven particular sacraments.

Third, the blessing extended by God through the created elements of the universe awaits a response. It is this offer and our response that together constitute the sacrament. Ritual sacraments of the Christian churches, Gibler argues, "are a continuation of the blessing and response that began at the birth of the Universe. All creation is potentially sacramental, and every being in creation has the potential to respond sacramentally to God's blessing."[3] This is true at the atomic and cellular levels, plant, sentient, and conscious human life. Each responds in the capacity of its specific nature and structure. Humanity has the unique capacity to respond in solidarity with all creation in the service of fullness of life because of our consciousness and self-consciousness. Through our ability to know about the rest of creation, we have the opportunity to recognize the offer of God in the grandeur of these myriad elements and to respond in faith. Sacramentality in our age has become cosmic.

Fourth, sacramentality that takes our materiality seriously and understands the mediation and embodiment of God in all created reality as gift includes an intrinsic connection with ethics. The bonds between humankind and the rest of the created universe are rooted in our common origins and destiny in Christ. This impels us to stand in solidarity with all persons who are marginalized and oppressed and with the environment of Earth that is currently experiencing oppression on a massive scale and to work for liberation and fullness of life. God's offer of self through the mediation of creation and those objects that are the work of human hands and our response to that offer cannot be separated from our care of those same material elements. The mutual relationality that characterizes the Trinity and the interdependence we are beginning to recognize in all creation suggests that our well-being can only be achieved through imitation of

---

[2] Ibid., vii.
[3] Ibid., xi.

that trinitarian love and recognition of our interdependence with all creation. We could also say that the individuality of the first Axial Period must give way to the relationality of the second Axial Period. Sacramentality is not simply meant to advance the relationship between the individual and the living God; it is tied to the mutual salvation of the whole cosmos.

It is helpful to look at some of the sacraments and see what the implications the new theology reviewed above may have on each of them. Let us first begin with baptism and confirmation, and then go on to consider eucharist and reconciliation.

Baptism/Confirmation

Traditionally we have spoken of baptism/confirmation as the sacraments which incorporate us into the Christ mystery. In light of our enlarged Christology, we can now suggest that the Christ in whom we have new life is the cosmic Christ, the One who is the source, life, and future of all creation. He is the one who summons us from ahead, who calls us to greater life and fullness. Christ is the symbol toward which humanity and the entire universe is evolving. He is the one who is immanent in creation and the Omega point toward which the universe is heading.

Our unity with Christ accomplished in the initiation sacraments ties us together not only with all Christians but with all humanity, indeed, with all creation. Christ is the source of our unity in the Body of Christ, but he is also the source of our unity with a cosmos that is related at every level, from the infinitesimally small to the largest dimension of the universe. In an emerging, complex world that is moving toward unity in diversity, Christ is the source and goal of that unity.

The Christian tradition since the time of Augustine has spoken of *sacramental character* as that dimension of our configuration to Christ that cannot be lost, unlike grace. The *character* with which we are marked in baptism and confirmation configures us to the *kenosis* of God in Christ. The kind of self-donation and self-offering of the cosmic Christ in service to the whole of creation is our model for fullness of life. His absolute fidelity to God's desire for the integrity and life of the whole universe engaged him especially with those who were marginalized, broken, or suffering in mind or body. Christ is the whole-maker; his solidarity with the marginalized led him on a ministry of reconciliation and healing of individuals and communities. His position as the cosmic Christ extends his ministry of whole-making to the universe as it emerges into the new. Absolute fidelity to this ministry is likewise meant for the baptized that are configured to Christ. As we have noted above, Jesus' ministry with the outcast led him into conflict with religious and political powers to the extent that he was put to death. Our *sacramental character* configures us to this Christ, and we cannot expect the fate of the Body to be significantly different from that of the Head.

We also noted that the new Christology stressed Christ's unity with the pains and suffering, joys, and happiness of the entire universe. Our relatedness to Christ engages us in solidarity with an evolving universe that is at once magnificent but also suffers through the evolutionary process of law and chance that is replete with struggle and death. We, no less than he, are called on to suffer and rejoice with all of created reality, for we are all kin by virtue of the interrelatedness of the universe and by virtue of our unity with Christ and in the power of the Holy Spirit. The new Christology engages us in the travails of our earthly environment particularly at this crisis moment in Earth's history when humankind finds itself so responsible for environmental degradation and ecocide. Our imitation of Christ carries with it an imperative for self-care, care for the rest of the human family, and particular care for our beleaguered planet and its non-human inhabitants.

Initiation into Christ not only configures us to Christ, it engages us on a lifelong quest for a profound spirituality, which is a precondition of our knowledge of Christ. This implies a life of deep engagement in the sacramental life of the church, communal and individual prayer, and praxis—all of which enable us to grow in knowledge and love of Christ. A community that is initiated into Christ is a community committed to participation in Christ, not just in the sacramental life of the church or in individual and communal prayer, but also in a cosmos. There is no dichotomy between matter and spirit, secular and religious; conversion and transformation of all in Christ is the goal of a truly sacramental life.

Earlier in this text I suggested that the West had emphasized Christology almost to the exclusion of Pneumatology. One of the helpful developments in the science and religion dialogue has been the return to a more robust theology of the Spirit. In fairness, interest in the proper role of the Holy Spirit was treated both immediately before and after the Second Vatican Council, and not all this work was connected to the dialogue with the New Sciences. However, by virtue of a combination of all these efforts, we are heir to a better balance between Christology and Pneumatology. This naturally has implications for a sacramental theology. In the *Rite of Christian Initiation of Adults,* paragraph 215, we hear of the desire for a better balance regarding the relationship between baptism and confirmation and between the mission of Christ and of the Spirit. The document reads:

> The conjunction of the two celebrations [baptism and confirmation] signifies the unity of the paschal mystery, the close link between the mission of the Son and the outpouring of the Holy Spirit, and the connection between the two sacraments through which the Son and the Holy Spirit come with the Father to those who are baptized.

The treatment of the Spirit in the *Rite of Confirmation* (*RC*) and in the *Apostolic Constitution on the Sacrament of Confirmation* (*AC*) emphasizes that the very essence of the sacrament is that "the faithful receive the Holy Spirit as a Gift" (*AC* 4). The effect of the gift of the Spirit is to "conform believers more perfectly to Christ" (*RC* 2), "anoint the candidates to be more like Christ the Son of God" (*RC* 24); the character of confirmation conforms the confirmed "more closely to Christ" (*RC* 9). The effect of the Spirit is also to empower for mission: "so that they may bear witness to Christ for the building up of his body in faith and love" (*RC* 2); the candidates are chrismated, which gives them "the grace of spreading the Lord's presence" (*RC* 9). The Opening Prayer of the Mass for Confirmation asks to send "the Holy Spirit [to] make us witnesses before the world to the Gospel of our Lord Jesus Christ." The gift of the Spirit also endows those being confirmed to "receive in increasing measure the treasures of divine life and advance toward the perfection of charity" (*AC* 1); they are "endowed . . . with [the] special strength [of the Holy Spirit]" (*AC* 8). Thus confirmation is an increase, a strengthening, a new degree of Christian life. Confirmation strengthens us in the Spirit for our baptismal commitment.

What would a renewed theology of the Holy Spirit contribute to a theology of confirmation? First of all, as Denis Edwards states, the

Spirit of God is more often now referred to as the Creator Spirit who graces all of existence. The Creator Spirit enabled the universe to exist from the beginning and holds everything in existence in all its emergence and fecundity. The *koinonia* that marks the relationship of the members of the Trinity one with another also marks the relationship of the Spirit with creation. This *koinonia* of the Spirit with all creation enlarges the concept of the Spirit's efforts at building up the church to building up unity with all of creation in all its diversity and complexity. Elizabeth Johnson stresses that the Spirit is the source of all life, renews the face of the earth, and moves throughout the cosmos. From here we can suggest that a renewed theology of the Spirit broadens the concept of the Spirit as presented in the confirmation rite and *Apostolic Constitution*. The Spirit not only strengthens the confirmandi but empowers the emergence of the more throughout the universe. The Creator Spirit, imaged as fire, wind, and water also conforms us to an even greater degree to Christ and his ministry, but the images now carry the valence of the first Flaring Forth, the solar winds, and the water that enables life on earth. Johnson's suggestion that we take seriously the personification of the Spirit of Wisdom in female form might lead us to be much more inclusive in our language for the Creator Spirit. In empowering the cosmos's emergence, She groans and midwifes the new; she vivifies and renews the face of the earth. It is this Spirit with which we are especially gifted in Confirmation.

Eucharist

Eucharist is the sacrament of the presencing of Christ in assembly, presider, word, and sacrament for those gathered in memory of him. It is the gift of a kenotic God of mutual relations who pours self out to achieve communion and transformation. Previously we have spoken of communion with Christ and one another as the end or the *res* of the eucharistic sacrament, but since the advent of the New Science we have come to a much deeper understanding of the relatedness of all in the universe. We must expand our imaginations to include in the communion of Christ those of other faith traditions and those who are not believers, as well as the community of Earth and the billions of galaxies that fill our skies. Christ is the Alpha of the universe; he is the new beginning, not the end. He is, as Ilia Delio says, "the New Creation, the New Being forming the horizon of a

new future, that is, the fullness of possibilities that lie before us."[4]
We who have been baptized/confirmed in Christ and the Spirit must
continue Christ's mission and that of the Holy Spirit. In an evolving
and emerging universe this means we must continue and advance
Jesus' work of whole-making. The sacrament of the eucharist is a
sacrament of new life and of the fullness of life in Christ. Through
participation in the eucharistic meal, we are not only configured to
Christ as in baptism/confirmation, we are literally made into Christ's
Body by partaking in his Body and Blood. We become divinized, as
our Eastern sisters and brothers would say. We become ever more
transformed into divine spirit that is the future of the universe. As
Delio says, "Baptism and Eucharist are sacraments of evolution that
empower the New Creation by forging new patterns of divine-human
relationship in the evolving cosmos."[5]

As I indicated above, the initiation sacraments of baptism and
confirmation configure us to Christ; eucharist does the same. We also
are called to live out a eucharistic life. By becoming bread for the
hungry and drink for the thirsty, we become part of the New Creation
symbolized by the Christ event and empowered by the Spirit. By
becoming sustenance for the planet, in ways we have yet to understand, we become new whole-makers for the universe. As a eucharistic people, we are called to create new webs of relationship in the
cosmos, participating thereby in the emergence of the New Creation.
Our model for doing this is a kenotic God of mutual relations who
suffers and rejoices with an emergent universe and the Christ who
is God's expression.

Eucharist is also about making anamnesis or memory of the great
salvific work of God in Jesus Christ. The point is not just to reminisce
about the past but to remember in such a way that the past becomes
present and the future is inaugurated. Christ is always the power of
the future—in this case, making-whole and uniting in new relationship with the divine. Anamnesis is also about tying the community
of remembrance into the salvific work of God in Christ. Through our
liturgical remembrance, we come to participate in that which we
remember. Eucharist links the Lord's Supper with his death and

---

[4] Ilia Delio, *The Emergent Christ* (Maryknoll, NY: Orbis Books, 2011), 98.
[5] Ibid., 99.

resurrection, thereby giving the eucharistic community a new mission—now, not just in the world as we know it, but in the universe. "The remembrance [of eucharist] is an empowerment to go and do the same: to die and rise in this new pattern of life at the heart of the universe that is the Christ."[6] Here death, which is an essential part of an evolving universe, takes on new meaning. Using our God-given freedom, we are called upon to pour ourselves out even unto death for the life of the universe, in expectation of the new life that is promised to us and that we remember in thanksgiving.

Eucharistic celebrations should be places where the Christian community is energized and empowered for its mission outside of liturgical space. Eucharistic communities should be communities committed to the transformation of patterns of separation and individualization into new patterns of relationship with the entire universe. In this second Axial Period, we are called to be ecologically sensitive, to have a global vision, and to be open to the expanse of the universe. Our sacraments can no longer be understood solely as a means of grace for the individual or for the developing relationship of the individual with God. Such private spirituality is too small for this second Axial Period. "What takes place in the Eucharist must sacramentalize our hope for the universe, union and transformation and a new future in God."[7]

Like all of the sacraments, the eucharist must be understood within the dynamic of divine offer and human response. This emphasis on the gift character of sacraments is writ large in the eucharist where, through the mediation of bread and cup, we receive the divine offer of Christ himself. But again, in light of the science/religion dialogue, we are coming to appreciate better that it is the Cosmic Christ whom we receive. Previously, eucharistic theology has stressed that we become what we receive, the Body of Christ (Augustine). However, we have understood the "Body of Christ" largely in ecclesial terms; we become ever more deeply the Body of Christ, the church. Our increased awareness of Christ as the Cosmic Christ has implications on our understanding of what we think we become in our eucharistic meal. Once again, our horizons are widened to become one with Him

---

[6] Ibid.
[7] Ibid., 100.

who is in solidarity with all humanity and with the whole universe. This certainly is a challenge to those who continue to hold a very individualistic theology and spirituality of the eucharist.

Reconciliation

This brings us to a consideration of reconciliation and of the sacrament of penance. I have deliberately begun with the word "reconciliation" because in the introduction to the *Rite of Penance* (*RP*) the sacraments of baptism and eucharist are rightly related to reconciliation with God and humanity before any treatment of the Sacrament of Penance is given. The Rite speaks of the "victory of Christ over sin" which is accomplished through a variety of means (*RP* 1): Jesus exhorted people to repentance, welcomed sinners, and reconciled them with the Father. In his ministry of healing, he often associated healing with reconciliation, exhorting men and women to "sin no more." The Rite speaks of Jesus "institut[ing] the sacrifice of the new covenant in his blood for the forgiveness of sins," "dy[ing] for our sins and [rising] for our justification" (*RP* 1). After his resurrection he sent the Holy Spirit to empower the apostles to forgive or retain sins. In the time of the church, Jesus' victory over sin is accomplished in the first place by the sacrament of baptism where "our fallen nature is crucified with Christ so that the body of sin may be destroyed and we may no longer be slaves to sin, but rise with Christ and live for God" (*RP* 2). In eucharist, the passion of Christ is made present and offered as "the sacrifice which has made our peace" with God and through which we may be brought together in unity (*RP* 2). In the sacrament of penance, Christ gave the church power to forgive sins after baptism and to be reconciled with God.

The church, which is always in need of conversion and repentance, accomplishes this ministry of reconciliation in a variety of ways as well: through uniting its sufferings with that of Christ and through its works of charity; through its expression in a life of reconciling acts with God and neighbor; through confession of sin which happens in prayer, worship, and the penitential aspects of the eucharistic celebration; through the sacrament of penance itself. In the tradition the church has always associated reconciliation with God, with reconciliation within the human community. This comes from the recognition that sin always involves an offense against God because of the unity of God with every person. Unfortunately, too often members of the church have sought reconciliation with God without seeking reconciliation with their neighbors and community as a corollary. In addition, in the first Axial Period, an individualistic approach to sin and to reconciliation reflected a narrow vision of relationship. Neither corporate sin nor corporate reconciliation has been on the forefront of the church's ministry of reconciliation to this point.

All of this is changing in this second Axial Period. Particularly since the end of the twentieth century, the corporate nature of sin has become an important focus of attention. Because of the multiple experiences of genocide, ethnic cleansing, and mass destruction that have marked this past century, the question of corporate conversion and reconciliation has come to the fore. Truth and reconciliation commissions in South Africa, Rwanda, and elsewhere have sought ways to address the tremendous amount of suffering and violence that has been visited upon whole communities and ethnic groups. Forgiveness and reconciliation are the aim, but are sought in response to at least an acknowledgment of the atrocities committed by individuals and groups. While churches have played a part in this ministry of reconciliation, the actual form of the sacrament of penance has not been affected by this shift in consciousness. The current Rite of Penance under form two (Rite for Reconciliation of Several Penitents) was drawn up to emphasize the relation of the sacrament to the community, but the date of the Rite's publication (1973) predated the growing recognition of corporate sin and the need for corporate reconciliation.

In light of the atrocities of our recent past, it is difficult to avoid the question: "Where was God amidst this massive suffering?" Elizabeth Johnson's efforts to answer this age-old question are helpful. Through the experience of Jesus' own suffering and death and in solidarity with the human community, God knows the suffering "from the inside" and does not abandon creation when in need. God is present to and with each individual and community as they undergo, in this case, humanly engendered violence. That presence does not eliminate the possibility of death or death itself, but in the resurrection of Christ, God promises that death will not have the last word.

A second dimension of the second Axial Period is the sensitivity toward Earth and the significant destruction that humankind has visited upon this planet. Relationship to the environment has now become a primary focus of attention. Earlier in the text I spoke about the new sense of solidarity between God and all creation and the subsequent expectation of solidarity of humankind with this beleaguered planet. The church needs to turn its attention to the conversion of its members to the sin of ecocide, to ecological responsibility, and to reconciliation with the planet and its myriad inhabitants. Only through such sensitivity and action can reconciliation with God be proclaimed.

Here too we can ask about God's solidarity with Earth in its travails and experiences of massive death, this time at the hands of the human community. Once again Johnson's suggestion that God suffers with creation and accompanies creation in the inevitable experience of death, either from natural or human causes, is helpful. God's solidarity with nonhuman creation demands no less from us in support of fullness of life and in reconciliation when we fail the planet. In terms of the ecocide we are experiencing in the beginning of the twenty-first century, the emphasis has to be on the corporate nature of our actions of sin and our efforts of reconciliation. While "deep incarnation" suggests God's solidarity with all creation, "deep resurrection" also promises transformation beyond death for all creation.

Overall, the church's ministry of reconciliation has been too narrowly construed regarding corporate sin and reconciliation vis-à-vis the human community with one another and the human community with Earth. The dialogue of science and religion has the potential for enlarging that vision and ministry. While we have made some attempts toward this end outside of ritual space, we have yet to transform our rituals of reconciliation in any of their permutations.

Chapter 7

Integrating the New Cosmology into Our Prayer Traditions

In addition to integrating the New Cosmology into our sacramental theology, how might we incorporate the insights of the science/religion *conversation* into our liturgical life? There are, in fact, many opportunities if we look at the whole compass of our liturgical practice. Creative persons could turn their attention to the liturgical calendar, prayer texts, liturgical song, and the environment for worship. Where traditions are open to modification, prayer texts could be changed in such a way as to broaden the range of experience that is addressed. As we have seen with our treatment of the sacraments, expanded notions of creation, God, Spirit, and Christology could be worked into already existing liturgical elements. In other cases, entirely new rituals could be created that take the science/religion *conversation* into account. In actuality, there have been some efforts made in both approaches that I will review, and I will include additional suggestions and possibilities. These suggestions are not official rites, but they serve as examples for communities that want to incorporate New Cosmology into their liturgical life.

Before addressing those particular topics, however, I would like to say a general word about the formative nature of liturgy and its ability to orient and reorient us vis-à-vis God, one another, and creation. As I noted above, our theology has become very anthropocentric in the last few centuries, and so too have our liturgies. They have had a two-pronged focus: our relation with God and with one another. Creation, if it is included at all, appears only in passing in some biblical readings and psalms.[1] Creation/Cosmos is not directly addressed as a "partner in praise,"[2] as the ground or source of human life, or as an object of our concern and need for reconciliation. If we are to reorient ourselves in right relation with Earth and the cosmos, then our liturgies must play a role in that reorientation. Liturgies can either serve to keep us alienated from or, at best, oblivious to created matter, or they can engender new patterns of relationship between ourselves and creation that are life-giving for all concerned. It is past time they did the latter.

Interestingly, the Bible is a rich source for understanding creation as a partner in praise with the human community, and so the intentional inclusion of pertinent passages would be helpful. Of course, Earth and its creatures praise God with the natural voices they have simply by being themselves, but the scriptures present them as subjects capable of sounding praise. Psalm 148 calls upon the sun and moon, shining stars, and waters above the heavens to join in praise of the God who created them. Sea monsters, mountains and hills, wild animals, creeping things, and flying birds are all implored to join in praise of the Creator. First Chronicles 16:31-36 is also rich in accounting for creation's praise: "Let the heavens be glad, and let the earth rejoice . . . Let the sea roar, and all that fills it; let the field exult, and everything in it. Then shall the trees of the forest sing for joy before the Lord." Using these texts more intentionally in newly created services that focus on creation, we can join our voices in solidarity with creation in our orientation of right relationship with God.

Creation raises its voice not only in praise but also in lament and in anguish. "The earth dries up and withers, the world languishes and withers; the heavens languish together with the earth" (Isa 24:4). Isaiah 33:9 likewise speaks of the anguish of the land: "The land mourns and

---

[1] An exception to this generalization is the reading of the Genesis 1 creation account at the Easter Vigil.

[2] I am indebted to Norman Habel for this phrase. See "Theology of Liturgy in a New Key: Worshiping with Creation," in *The Season of Creation: A Preaching Commentary*, ed. Norman Habel, David Rhoads, and Paul Santmire (Minneapolis, MN: Fortress Press, 2010), 4. Chapter 2 of this text, "Theology of Liturgy in a New Key: Worshiping with Creation," is available online at http://www.letallcreationpraise.org/theology-of-worship; accessed April 4, 2013. It is this source that I used.

languishes; Lebanon is confounded and withers away; Sharon is like a desert; and Ba'shan and Car'mel shake off their leaves." Jeremiah also speaks of the plight of the created world: "How long will the land mourn, and the grass of every field wither?" (Jer 12:4). The prophet Joel speaks too of the pain of the earth and its creatures: "How the animals groan. . . . Even the wild animals cry to you because the watercourses are dried up" (Joel 1:18, 20). In the first Testament, these tragedies befell creation because of Israel's infidelity to the covenant,[3] but few if any preachers extend this lesson to our own day or join these prophets in a call to accountability and conversion.

In our age, it is often because of human behavior that Earth shrivels and dries up through destruction of habitats and of the ecological balance that Earth has developed over the millennia. Human solidarity with Earth and its creatures calls us to accountability not only for the sake of nature—which is a worthy project in and of itself—but for the destruction of nature that prevents it from being a partner with us in praise of God. Could not our liturgies exhibit human solidarity with Earth and its creatures in acts of praise and lament as a daily event? As Norman Habel asks, "Can we then worship in ways that enable us to lament with other creatures as well as to celebrate with them, and to express our responsibility toward them? If we will do so, only then will we truly join them in worship with integrity, as the God we know in the Bible intends us to do."[4]

Some biblical texts also ground the human person in Earth and establish us as kin to everything else. A fresh reading of the creation account of Genesis 2 would hopefully lead us in this direction. We hear that the first human (ʿādām) is created from the dust of the earth, from the soil (ʿădāmāh) of Earth (Gen 2:7). So too did God make the plants rise from Earth (Gen 2:9) and every animal and bird was formed from Earth as a companion to ʿādām (Gen 2:19). God placed ʿādām in the garden God had created to "till it and keep it" (Gen 2:15). Indeed all creatures—humanity, the plants and animals—are all drawn from Earth and are given life through God's breath. We

---

[3] See Dianne Bergant, *The Earth Is the Lord's: The Bible, Ecology, and Worship* (Collegeville, MN: Liturgical Press, 1998), 39–40.

[4] Habel, "Theology of Worship," 10. http://www.letallcreationpraise.org/theology -of-worship; accessed April 4, 2013.

share a common source, and we also share a common destiny. Paul tells us in Romans 8:19, 21 that creation "waits with eager longing for the revealing of the children of God . . . in hope that the creation itself will be set free from its bondage to decay and will obtain the freedom of the glory of the children of God." If we read these passages with an eye toward our common heritage and a common future, they have the potential for opening our imaginations to the interdependence we have with Earth and its creatures.

As Elizabeth Johnson has reminded us, we must not romanticize nature, since even without human intervention the earth is filled with tremendous suffering, destruction, and death. The question of God's relationship to this suffering is a profound question that requires deep pondering and personal prayer. This too must be addressed in our worship, our corporate prayer, because it is an important force in shaping our understanding of God and in framing profound questions. The reflections of Johnson and others on this topic of cosmic suffering must be woven into the prayer texts, the music and the environment of our liturgical celebrations.

Our worship needs to join with creation's praise and lament not only on distinct days (e.g., Earth Day) but in every liturgy and in all seasons. Only through such a thoroughgoing process will we be able to move from our anthropocentrism to a more integrated appreciation of the relationship of God with humanity and all creation. Only by attending to the "turn to the cosmos" in all aspects of our liturgical prayer will the liturgies be able to do their formative work on us, and convert us to care for Earth and its creatures outside of liturgical space. Nonetheless, before we transform all of our worship, we might begin by making changes in small but deliberate ways. The following are some suggestions of what we might do.

The Liturgical Calendar

Too often we have considered celebrating the cosmic cycles of the seasons, of winter and summer solstice, as remnants of pagan religious practice, and from which Christianity needs to distance itself. In the current context, such an approach and attitude needs to be overturned. As I indicated in chapter 1, in the second Axial Period we must take the wisdom of those in the pre-Axial and first Axial

Periods and add it to the insights of our present age. Attending to the natural cycles of our solar system could be an invitation to see all of reality as "God-drenched," as Linda Gibler suggests. This is an opportunity to be delighted and to be filled with awe in the revelation of divine disclosure in the environment which shapes our days, nights, and years. Such an approach to God's creative action and God's own delight in creation has strong roots in the biblical tradition, but our current understanding of the New Cosmology extends that biblical insight further than anything imagined before. The "turn to the cosmos" is an opportunity to extend our imaginations and our ethics to include the whole universe in our concerns. It is also an opportunity to celebrate the interrelatedness and interdependence of all reality. In the relational model of existence outlined above, there is not the sacred and the profane; instead, all exists in God and all expresses God's desire to share self. Human dominance over the nonhuman is excluded, for all of creation has rights (not the same rights as human beings, but rights nonetheless). Even language of human stewardship over creation needs to be modified in recognition of the interdependence of created reality. Too often stewardship presumes a relationship of superiority of the human *over* nature, an attitude that can no longer be maintained.

In the current liturgical dispensation, the temporal calendar is used almost exclusively to honor the salvation history story of God in Jesus Christ and in the power of the Spirit. This makes the celebration of the liturgical year an act of anamnesis, inviting participation in the reality signified. Using the calendar to honor creation (original, continual, new) would perhaps limit our androcentrism and force us to take more account of and show more gratitude for, the rest of creation. We would need to take care to honor the elements of creation "in themselves alone," and not just in how they can be useful to the human community. We can also rejoice in their ability to disclose the divine *kenosis* which is itself an act of loving concern for creation that includes the human community. This "turn to the cosmos" would also contextualize the story of divine disclosure of the Word in Jesus Christ.

What would this look like? I am imagining that we could create a feast that would celebrate the first Flaring Forth (instead of the rather inelegant "Big Bang") of the universe some 13.8 billion years ago.

A second feast might celebrate the emergence of our galaxy and the formation of our solar system. Another could mark the emergence of life on planet Earth. A fourth could celebrate the emergence of human life from our hominid ancestors. (In spite of the fact that we do not know the exact time or manner of the emergence of mind, we do know there is a qualitative difference in our consciousness and self-consciousness from our primate ancestors.) We might also celebrate the development of language and the harnessing of fire. Each of these moments is of enormous importance, and we would do well to honor them with liturgical celebrations.

The relationship of humanity with Earth and its creatures also needs to be taken into account, and this too could be integrated into the liturgical seasons. A movement has begun simultaneously in many countries to celebrate the various aspects of Earth, the relationship of humanity with Earth and its creatures, and the need for reconciliation and healing with Earth.[5] The Episcopal Church has already moved in this direction. In the mid-1990s, they began a four-week *Season of Creation*, which could be celebrated at any point in the liturgical year but which they found most appropriately placed during the Season of Pentecost. Other churches celebrate the *Season of Creation* from September 1 through October 4, the feast of St. Francis of Assisi. The Lutheran church has also adopted this seasonal plan, creating a three-year cycle of themes and biblical readings according to the lectionary plan of the *Revised Common Lectionary* (Matthew, Mark, and Luke). Year A includes Sundays that honor "Forest," "Land," "Wilderness," and "River"; Year B includes "Planet Earth," "Humanity," "Sky," "Mountain," and "Blessing of Animals"; and Year C includes "Ocean," "Fauna," "Storm," and "Cosmos/Universe."[6] A strong ecological sensitivity is built into this seasonal plan, with room for not only praise of creation but repentance by humanity for the destruction of our earthly home, and with a man-

---

[5] See Habel, Rhoads, and Santmire, *The Season of Creation*, 7–9, for an account of the development of this movement.

[6] See the following website for a wealth of material on celebrating the *Season of Creation*. This is sponsored by the Web of Creation at the Lutheran School of Theology, Chicago, http://www.webofcreation.org; accessed April 1, 2013. Among the resources provided is a list of websites for what each of the mainline denominations is doing. For Roman Catholic resources see http://catholicclimatecovenant.org.

date to address the ecological concerns voiced in the service outside the worship space.

Prayer Texts

As I indicated above, we need to pay attention to already existing prayer texts and to the creative composition of new ones, as well as to the creation of whole services that would honor an evolutionary and ecological worldview. One can hope that the Christian churches would make attempts at creating new eucharistic prayers in light of the areas spoken of above: God's original and ongoing creativity, God's and our solidarity with all creation, and the redemption of the universe. A "Call to Worship" for Universe Sunday gives a taste of what could be created for a prayer service or eucharist:

Call to Worship

L1 We invite all creation to worship with us.
P We invite glittering galaxies high in the sky
to radiate the splendor of God's presence.

L2 We call distant domains of space to celebrate with us.
P We invite nebula, nova, and red giant stars
to thank God for their formation in the universe.

L3 We summon that domain of stardust called Earth,
P To pulse with the rhythm of God's presence
and celebrate God's glory in this planet garden.

L1 We invite millions of living species to dance with life,
P The turtle, the toad, and the elephant,
the earthworm, the ant and the dragonfly.

L2 We invite every creature in the web of creation
P To consciously connect with others
in this cosmic community called the universe.

L3 Dance, creation, dance!
P Dance with life and cosmic energy![7]

---

[7] See this entire service at http://www.webofcreation.org/season-of-creation /liturgical-cycle-c/59-universe-sunday; accessed April 4, 2013.

New collects and new prefaces would need to be prepared, should new feasts be added to the calendar. A possible collect for the birth of the universe would be the following:

> Blessed are You, Holy God of all that was, is, and ever shall be!
> In your goodness and infinite generosity
> you poured yourself out into creation,
> from the first flaring forth of matter and energy
> to this very day.
> Open our eyes in awe at the wonder of the universe,
> turn our hearts to gratitude
> for your ongoing work of creation,
> and awaken our hope
> for the dream of a new creation
> when You shall be all in all.
>
> We ask this in the name of Jesus Christ
> and in the power of the Creator Spirit.[8]

Present collects could be modified to take into account the developments in a more relational understanding of God and in an ecological theology. The Lutheran tradition has a preface for "Universe Sunday" in cycle C of the *Season of Creation* that reads as follows:[9]

> L The Creator be with you and with all creation.
> **P And also with you.**
>
> L Open your hearts.
> **P We open them to our Creator.**
>
> L Let us give thanks to our Creator.
> **P It is right to join the universe in thanking God.**
>
> L God our Creator,
> source of everything in the universe,
> we bring before you this day,
> bread and wine
> and with it we bring before you the whole creation to say:
> **P Thank you, God, thank you!**

---

[8] Written by the author.
[9] Available at http://www.webofcreation.org/season-of-creation/liturgical -cycle-c/59-universe-sunday; accessed April 4, 2013.

L Thank you for joining the web of creation
for living and dying among us
to redeem us and all creation:
P Thank you, God, thank you!

L Thank you for rising to life
permeating the universe with your Spirit
to sustain and heal all things:
P Thank you, God, thank you!

L Therefore with voices of thanks
echoing through the universe
from the first day of creation
until this very moment in time,
we praise and thank you saying:

**P Holy! Holy! Holy! Lord God of all life!
All creation is filled with your presence!**

Prefaces are provided for each of the Sundays of the entire three-year cycle and are available at the same website listed above.[10] Such prayers could raise the consciousness of the celebrating communities, and, hopefully, lead to new praxis, particularly regarding the ecological crisis we are facing.

I have written a full Eucharistic Prayer in the Roman Catholic tradition that could be used at any of the new feasts that I have suggested. It reads as follows:

Introductory Dialogue:
Lift up your hearts;
R. We lift them up to the Creator of the Cosmos.
Let us give thanks to our God;
R. It is right and just.

Preface
It is truly right and just to bless you, God of the Cosmos,
and to praise you for your glory.
Before time and matter existed, you were,
from everlasting to everlasting.
In a desire to share yourself,

---

[10] http://www.webofcreation.org/season-of-creation/; accessed February 17, 2014.

you willed the cosmos into being.
In one great flaring forth,
light, time, and mass appeared.
The mighty forces of gravity and nuclear energy came to be.
Vast clouds of gases, dust, and stars emerged;
Galaxies, black holes, dark energy, and matter
spiraled outward with ever-increasing speed.

But galaxies, stars, and nebulas were not enough for you.
In your goodness, you brought forth planets
—like our beloved Earth—where life could thrive.
You dreamed of living beings
who would share your breath, and grow and multiply.
So life began—algae and ferns came forth;
then animals of every description filled the land and sea.
One day human persons emerged, created in your image,
gifted with consciousness and filled with grace.

We grew in awareness of you,
author and sustainer of life,
and sought ways to respond to you.
We often failed to return your love,
but you never ceased to draw us to yourself.
In covenant after covenant, you reached out to us
seeking our friendship and love.
You sent prophets, courageous women and men,
who called us to fidelity as your beloved people.

And so with all the angels and the saints,
with the cosmos in all its variety
we lift our voices in praise.

Holy, holy, holy . . .

Out of your immense love for us,
you sent your eternal Word, Sophia/Wisdom,
to join our human community,
becoming like us in all ways but sin.
Your Word so entered into created time and history
that He shared in our dreams and hopes, joys, and sufferings.
He revealed your reign in his passion
for justice, peace, and communion with all creation.

He gave Himself to us as a sign of your love,
but was given over to the forces of sin and death.

Epiclesis

We pray that you would send your Spirit
upon this bread and cup that they may become for us
His life-giving body and blood,
a sign of the new and everlasting covenant.

Institution Narrative

Knowing that His time on earth was coming to a close,
He gathered his disciples together in a covenant meal.
He took bread, blessed it, and said to those gathered:
Take and eat of this, all of you;
this is my body which is given for you.

Likewise, after the supper,
he took the cup and giving thanks said:
Take and drink, all of you;
this is my blood which shall be shed for you and for all
for forgiveness of sins.
Do this in memory of me.

Faith Acclamation

Anamnesis and Epiclesis

Therefore, remembering his union in death with us and all things,
his resurrection which is our hope, his ascension to your right hand,
and awaiting his coming again, we offer you these gifts,
the bread of life and the cup of salvation,
gifts bestowed in love, and now returned to you.
Through your Holy Spirit, join us in communion with you,
and with all the created world.

Intercessions

Remember the suffering of the cosmos and
of all your creatures here on Earth.
Help us to trust that you hold all things in love
in ways that exceed our understanding.
Remember your church; give it unity and wisdom.

Strengthen your people to love as you love,
and to care for all with whom we share this cosmos.

Doxology

Attempts at revising existing texts in Roman Catholicism have begun to happen, but on a small scale. In the mid-1990s, the International Commission on English in the Liturgy (ICEL), when it was still able to consider original texts, put forth a revised Exsultet intended for the Easter Vigil in the new Sacramentary. It was never officially accepted or published, but it shows an initial attempt at being more cosmologically conscious. I am including part of it here as an example of what might be done.

We praise you, God, for all your works of light!
We bless you for that burst of fire and flame
through which you first created all that is:
a living universe of soaring stars,
of space and spinning planets, surging seas
that cradle earth and rock against her breast. . . .

We bless you for the light invisible:
the fire of faith, the Spirit's grace and truth,
the light that bonds the atom, stirs the heart,
and shines for ever on the face of Christ!

In this text the triumphant story of Christ's victory over death is couched in the larger story of the cosmos. Much more could be done, but as an initial effort, this was an admirable start.

In her text *From the Beginning to Baptism*, Linda Gibler writes three blessings/hymns on the main symbols of baptism: water, oil, and fire. I include the one on water here because it is a much more fulsome effort at contextualizing the salvation history story within the cosmic history of water.

Blessed are you, Ever-Present God,
    Creator of the Universe,
    Through you we have the gift of water for baptism.
Water that formed in the remnants of ancient stars
    and brought our Day Star to birth.

Water that cooled the nascent Earth.
    Rising from deep within and carried by comets,
    your water drenched our young planet
    and covered it in oceans.
Water that birthed the first life on Earth
    and each life thereafter
    Water that fills and flows within every living being.

This water of Stars, Earth, and Life you give
    to bring us into fullness of life in you.
This is the water over which your Spirit hovered at the Beginning,
    the water that cleansed the Earth in Noah's day,
    through which the Israelites passed unharmed
    in Moses' day,
    and in which Jesus was baptized.

This is the water Jesus calmed,
    the water he turned into wine in Cana,
    and that flowed from his side on Calvary.

Ever-Present God, your Spirit continuously moves within water.
    Enliven the water in this font and in us
    so we may remember that all water flows
    with your holy presence.

Blessed are you, Ever-Present God,
    Creator of the Universe,
    Through you we have the gift of water for baptism.[11]

The possibilities of prayers that take the New Cosmology into account are endless. These examples are simply to give a taste of what is possible.

Liturgical Song

Within all of our traditions the place that is the most flexible and has the greatest capacity to incorporate changing concerns into the liturgy is hymnody. During the time of the Reformation and thereafter, the

---

[11] Linda Gibler, *From the Beginning to Baptism: Scientific and Sacred Stories of Water, Oil, and Fire* (Collegeville, MN: Liturgical Press, 2010), 1–2.

Episcopal and Protestant traditions found ample opportunity within song to express their distinct identities and their theological values. One need only look at Luther and his work with hymnody, the psalm tradition in Calvinism, and the eucharistic texts of the Methodist Charles Wesley to find convincing evidence of the power of song. Roman Catholicism has done similar things historically and in recent times. It has been through the work of composers and lyricists after Vatican II that Roman Catholics have come to appropriate the scriptures and to express the social justice legacy of the Catholic Church. We need our wordsmiths to do a similar ministry regarding an evolutionary and ecological theology.

The following text by Marty Haugen gives an indication of what might be done in a text honoring the Spirit. While the stress is more on Earth, one could read into the text references to the whole cosmos.

Spirit blowing through creation,
Spirit burning in the skies,
Let hope of your salvation fill our eyes;
God of splendor, God of glory,
You who light the stars above,
All the heavens tell the story of your love.

Refrain:
Spirit renewing the earth,
Renewing the hearts of all people;
Burn in the weary souls,
blow through the silent lips,
come now awake us, Spirit of God.

As you moved upon the waters,
As you ride upon the wind,
Move us all, your sons and daughters, deep within;
As you shaped the hills and mountains,
Formed the land and filled the deep,
Let your hand renew and waken all who sleep.

Love that sends the rivers dancing,
Love that waters all that lives,
Love that heals and holds and rouses and forgives;
You are food for all your creatures,

You are hunger in the soul,
In your hands the broken-hearted are made whole.

All the creatures you have fashioned,
All that live and breathe in you,
Find their hope in your compassion, strong and true;
You, O Spirit of salvation,
You alone, beneath, above,
Come renew your whole creation in your love.[12]

The Lutheran Norman Habel has an entire hymnal devoted to songs that take the New Cosmology into account. Here is one composed for the Feast of St. Francis of Assisi, published on the Web of Creation website. The melody is the well-known hymn *Praise My Soul, the King of Heaven.*

1. Mother Earth, our mother birthing
   Ev'ry creature on the land
   Jesus too was flesh and breathing,
   Kin to every greening plant.
   Celebrate with all creation:
   God has joined the web of life.

2. Sister Air, our sister lifting
   Ev'ry creature born with wing;
   Jesus shared the breath of forests,
   Breath that makes our spirits sing.
   Celebrate with all creation:
   God has joined the web of life.

3. Brother Water, brother pulsing
   Deep through ev'ry vein and sea,
   Jesus drank the very raindrops
   For our wine and in our tea.
   Celebrate with all creation:
   God has joined the web of life.

4. Father Fire, our father burning
   With the sacred urge to live.

---

[12] Marty Haugen, "Spirit Blowing Through Creation" (Chicago: GIA Publications, 1987). Used with permission.

Jesus' death completes the cycle,
Bringing life beyond the grave.
Celebrate with all creation:
God has joined the web of life.[13]

Environment

Liturgical architects and artists also can play a key role in shaping the imagination of the liturgical assembly. Whether in the design of church and synagogue spaces or the decoration of the same, architects and artists create environments through which we conceive of God, our relationship with divine mystery, and our relationship to the cosmos. If images of Earth from outer space have had a profound effect on our culture, so too have the images of the universe provided by the Hubble Spacecraft, and the electron microscope broadened and deepened our appreciation for God's creation. We await those gifted artists among us who will translate these images into glass, steel and stone, color, light, and texture. For liturgies such as those suggested for a *Season of Creation*, it is recommended that the environment include examples of the domains emphasized on each Sunday. Those churches with electronic capabilities to project images in the worship space could include presentations of photographs of those domains in question. Opening ritual spaces out into their surrounding environments also would help in building appreciation of our Earthly habitat, but that would need to be joined to liturgies that more intentionally focus our attention on the human/creation relationship.

New Rituals

Innumerable new rituals have been created by various church communities on topics of ecological justice. These new rituals include raising consciousness to the beauties of creation, confession of the sin of ecocide and the destruction of habitats, and commitment for

---

[13] Norman Habel, "Mother Earth, Our Mother Birthing," taken from the Habel Hymnal, vol. 1, 1999. Published on http://www.webofcreation.org/season-of -creation/liturgical-cycle-b/55-blessing-of-the-animals; accessed April 4, 2013.

much needed stewardship of Earth. The United States Conference of Catholic Bishops has several resources available for study and prayer on the issues of ecology and climate change.[14] Other organizations also have made worship resources available online for use by faith communities.

The following newly composed prayer service could be celebrated on the feast of the Birthing of the Universe or at another time.[15] It is intended as an evening service, generally following the form of Evening Prayer in the Liturgy of the Hours. This traditional form is used in order to give the assembly a sense of security even while the content of the service introduces ideas and images that might stretch the community's imagination.

Evening Prayer for the Feast of the Birthing of the Cosmos

Environment

In darkness and silence someone with a Fire Pot processes in and sets it on a pedestal. After a few moments of silence the lights are turned slightly up and the gathering song is sung.

Gathering Song
God, Who Stretched the Spangled Heavens (Hymn tune: Ode to Joy)

1 God, who stretched the spangled heavens, infinite in time and
       place,
    flung the suns in burning radiance through the silent fields of
       space,
    we your children, in your likeness, share inventive powers with
       you.
    Great Creator, still creating, show us what we yet may do.

---

[14] See, for example: Thomas G. Wenski and Nicholas DiMarzio, *Faithful Stewards of God's Creation: A Catholic Resource for Environmental Justice and Climate Change* (Washington, DC: USCCB Publishing, 2007); and *Global Climate Change: A Plea for Dialogue, Prudence, and the Common Good*, A Statement of the United States Conference of Catholic Bishops, June 15, 2001.

[15] I am grateful to Mary Henry, CCVI, and Cathy Vetter, CCVI, for their help in creating this ritual.

2 We have conquered worlds undreamed of since the childhood of
    our race;
  known the ecstasy of winging through uncharted realms of space;
  probed the secrets of the atom, yielding unimagined power,
  facing us with life's destruction or our most triumphant hour.

3 As each far horizon beckons, may it challenge us anew,
  children of creative purpose, serving others, honoring you.
  May our dreams prove rich with promise, each endeavor well begun;
  Great Creator, give us guidance till our goal and yours are one.[16]

Call to Worship

Leader: God of the cosmos, source of all life, love, and blessing.
Assembly: **We glorify you, we rejoice in you.**
Leader: Jesus Christ, the Word incarnate, Savior of all that ever
           was, is and will be.
Assembly: **We glorify you, we rejoice in you.**
Leader: Creator Spirit, throbbing and pulsing throughout time
           and eternity.
Assembly: **We glorify you, we rejoice in you.**

Opening Prayer:

Gathered this night in prayer and praise, we take time to remember God's infinite mercy and goodness in creating the cosmos. Triune God, living in inexhaustible light and love, be with us this night to open our eyes in wonder at your creation and enflame our hearts with gratitude. We ask this and all things through your Word and in the power of your Spirit.

Psalmody: Psalm 89

Antiphon: I will sing of your steadfast love forever.
I will sing of your steadfast Love
forever, my Beloved;
  with forthright voice I will proclaim
your goodness to all generations.
For your abiding Love rules the universe,
  your faithfulness extends throughout
the firmament.

[16] Catherine Cameron, "God Who Stretched the Spangled Heavens" (Carol Stream, IL: Hope Publishing Co., 1967). All rights reserved. Used by permission.

Your Covenant from the beginning of time
   encompasses all who choose to walk
the path of Love;
And to all generations that honor
your Way and your Truth,
   will Love make Itself known.

Antiphon: I will sing of your steadfast love forever.

Let the heavens praise your wonders,
O Loving Creator,
   your faithfulness in the congregation
of the holy ones!
For who in the universe is comparable
to You?
   Who among the heavenly beings
is like You—
You, who are reverenced in the council
of the holy ones,
   great in wisdom, gentle of heart, and
one with all around You.
O Most High, mighty are You,
   whose Grace is poured forth
throughout all ages.[17]

Antiphon: I will sing of your steadfast love forever.

Psalm Prayer

Creator God, blessed are you for your goodness to us and all creation. You have shared yourself with us in unspeakable generosity. The heavens are filled with your glory; our hearts are filled praise. Keep us mindful of our responsibility in caring for Earth and all its creatures.

Psalm 148

Antiphon: Praise the Blessed One!

Praise the Blessed One!
Give praise from the heavens,
   and from all the ends of the earth!

---

[17] Nan C. Merrill, *Psalms for Praying: An Invitation to Wholeness* (New York: Continuum, 2008), 175.

Give praise all you angels,
   angels of earth and of heaven!

Give praise sun and moon,
   give praise, all you shining stars!
Give praise, all universes,
   the whole cosmos of Creation!

Antiphon: Praise the Blessed One!

Praise the Blessed One!
   For through Love all was created
And firmly fixed for ever and ever;
   Yes, the pattern of creation
was established.

Give praise to the Beloved,
all the earth,
   all that swim in the deep,
And all the winged ones in the air!
Give praise all mountains and hills,
   all trees and all minerals!
Give praise all four-legged
   and all that creep on the ground!

Antiphon: Praise the Blessed One!

Leaders of the nations and all peoples,
young and old,
Give praise! Unite together in all
your diversity,
   that peace and harmony might
      flourish on earth!

Let all people praise the Beloved,
   who is exalted in heaven and
on earth;
   whose glory is above heaven and earth.

Antiphon: Praise the Blessed One!

For all are called to be friends,
   companions to the true Friend,
   giving their lives joyfully as

co-creators and people
   of peace!
Praise be to the blessed One,
   the very Breath of our breath,
   the very Heart of our heart![18]

Antiphon: Praise the Blessed One!

Psalm Prayer

Praised be to you who are the source and joy of all creation! Keep us mindful of our unity with all your creatures and all peoples so that we may live in peace and harmony.

Reading: "Genesis for the Third Millennium"[19]

There was God. And God was All-That-Was. God's Love overflowed and God said, 'Let Other be. And let it have the capacity to become what it might be, making it make itself—and let it explore its potentialities.'

   And there was Other in God, a field of energy, vibrating energy—but no matter, space, time or form. Obeying its given laws and with one intensely hot surge of energy—a hot big bang—this Other exploded as the universe from a point twelve or so billion years ago in our time, thereby making space.

   Vibrating fundamental particles appeared, expanded and expanded, and cooled into clouds of gas, bathed in radiant light. Still the universe went on expanding and condensing into swirling whirlpools of matter and light—a billion galaxies.

   Five billion years ago, one star in one galaxy—our Sun—became surrounded by matter as planets. One of them was our Earth. On Earth, the assembly of atoms and the temperature became just right to allow water and solid rack to form. Continents and mountains grew and in some deep wet crevice, or pool, or deep in the sea, just over three billion years ago some molecules became large and complex enough to make copies of themselves and became the first specks of life.

   Life multiplied in the seas, diversifying and becoming more and more complex. Five hundred million years ago, creatures with solid

---

[18] Ibid., 294–95.
[19] Arthur Peacocke, *Paths from Science towards God: The End of All Our Exploring* (Oxford, UK: Oneworld, 2001), 1–2.

skeletons—the vertebrates—appeared. Algae in the sea and green plant on land changed the atmosphere by making oxygen. Then three hundred million years ago, certain fish learned to crawl from the sea and live on the edge of land, breathing that oxygen from the air.

Now life burst into many forms—reptiles, mammals (and dinosaurs) on land—reptiles and birds in the air. Over millions of years the mammals developed complex brains that enabled them to learn. Among these were creatures who lived in trees. From these our first ancestors derived and then, only forty thousand years ago, the first men and women appeared. They began to know about themselves and what they were doing—they were not only conscious but also self-conscious. The first word, the first laugh were heard. The first paintings were made. The first sense of a destiny beyond—with the first signs of hope, for these people buried their dead with ritual. The first prayers were made to the One who made All-That-Is and All-That-Is-Becoming—the first experiences of goodness, beauty and truth—but also of their opposites, for human beings were free.

Silence

Singing Bowl Marks the End of the Silence

Presider Invites Spontaneous Prayers of Gratitude from the Assembly
I am grateful for the Milky Way Galaxy that fills the night sky with
    shimmering light!
I am grateful for the caterpillars and butterflies that show us the
    possibilities of transformation!
I am grateful . . .

Closing Prayer
Creating and sustaining God, you bless us with the wonders of the universe and give us the gift of joy in your presence. Keep us ever grateful for your love and care, and enable us to be cocreators with you in bringing justice and peace to our beloved Earth. We ask this and all things through your Word and in the power of your Spirit.

Blessing and Dismissal:
L: May the Holy One sustain you in love.
Assembly: Amen
L: May the only-begotten Word guide you in all truth.
Assembly: Amen

L: May the Spirit encourage you in faith.
Assembly: Amen

L: Let us go in peace.
Assembly: Thanks be to God.

Environment: The leader takes the still burning fire pot and processes out with it.

Conclusion

It is clear from all that has been said that the task of integrating the science/religion dialogue into our worship patterns and prayers is immense. Those churches whose worship patterns are more flexible will have an easier time in incorporating new feasts, new liturgical seasons, and new prayers. Those communions such as the Roman Catholic Church, whose approval process for new liturgies and new texts is quite elaborate and slow, will have a more difficult time in integrating this new paradigm shift. Nonetheless, there is room for services created on an *ad hoc* basis and for the development of hymnody and environments that take these cosmic and ecological concerns into account. Despite the difficulties and obstacles that may come up, I am convinced the effort must be made to address this paradigm shift. The immediate ecological issues are too pressing for us to delay any longer. The integration of cosmic consciousness is a larger issue that will take generations to accomplish, but it is still an important task that faces us in our own generation.

Recommended Reading

Barbour, Ian. *Religion in an Age of Science*. San Francisco: Harper & Row, 1990; revised and expanded as *Religion and Science*, 1997.

Berry, Thomas. *The Dream of the Earth*. San Francisco: Sierra Club Books, 1988.

Boff, Leonardo. *Cry of the Earth, Cry of the Poor*. Maryknoll, NY: Orbis Books, 1997.

Delio, Ilia. *Christ in Evolution*. Maryknoll, NY: Orbis Books, 2008.

———. *The Emergent Christ: Exploring the Meaning of Catholic in an Evolutionary Universe*. Maryknoll, NY: Orbis Books, 2011.

Edwards, Denis. *Breath of Life: A Theology of the Creator Spirit*. Maryknoll, NY: Orbis Books, 2004.

———. *Creation, Humanity, Community: Building a New Theology*. Dublin: Gill and Macmillan Ltd., 1992.

———. *How God Acts: Creation, Redemption, and Special Divine Action*. Minneapolis, MN: Fortress Press, 2010.

———. *Jesus and the Evolving Cosmos*. Eugene, OR: Wipf and Stock, 2004.

Fragomeni, Richard N., and John T. Pawlikowski, eds. *The Ecological Challenge: Ethical, Liturgical, and Spiritual Responses*. Collegeville, MN: Liturgical Press, 1994.

Gregersen, Niels, and Wentzel van Huyssteen, eds. *Rethinking Theology and Science: Six Models for the Current Dialogue*. Grand Rapids, MI: Eerdmans, 1998.

Haught, John. *Christianity and Science: Toward a Theology of Nature*. Mary-knoll, NY: Orbis Books, 2007.

———. *God after Darwin: A Theology of Evolution*, 2nd Edition. Boulder CO: Westview Press, 2008.

———. *Science and Religion: From Conflict to Conversation*. Mahwah, NJ: Paulist Press, 1995.

Hays, Zachary. *A Window to the Divine: Creation Theology*. Quincy, IL: Franciscan Press, 1997.

Hessel, Dieter T., and Rosemary Radford Ruether, eds. *Christianity and Ecology: Seeking the Well-Being of Earth and Humans*. Cambridge, MA: Harvard University Press, 2000.

Johnson, Elizabeth A. *Ask the Beasts: Darwin and the God of Love*. London: Bloomsbury, 2014.

———. *She Who Is: The Mystery of God in Feminist Theological Discourse*. New York: Crossroad, 1992.

———. *Women, Earth, and Creator Spirit*. Mahwah, NJ: Paulist Press, 1993.

Lathrop, Gordon. *Holy Ground: A Liturgical Cosmology*. Minneapolis, MN: Fortress Press, 2003.

Mick, Laurence E. *Liturgy and Ecology in Dialogue*. Collegeville, MN: Liturgical Press, 1997.

Peacocke, Arthur. *Paths from Science towards God: The End of All Our Exploring*. Oxford, UK: OneWorld, 2001.

Santmire, H. Paul. *Ritualizing Nature: Renewing Christian Liturgy in a Time of Crisis*. Minneapolis, MN: Fortress Press, 2008.

Schaab, Gloria L. *The Creative Suffering of the Triune God*. New York: Oxford University Press, 2007.

———. *Trinity in Relation: Creation, Incarnation, and Grace in an Evolving Cosmos*. Winona, MN: Anselm Academic, 2012.

Southgate, Christopher. *The Groaning of Creation: God, Evolution, and the Problem of Evil*. Louisville, KY: Westminster John Knox, 2008.

Swimme, Brian, and Thomas Berry. *The Universe Story: From the Primordial Flaring Forth to the Ecozoic Era: A Celebration of the Unfolding of the Cosmos*. San Francisco: Harper, 1992.

Index